*Marketing on a Small Budget*

# Marketing on a Small Budget

Edited by Christopher West
*Deputy Managing Director*
*Industrial Market Research Limited*

Associated Business Programmes
LONDON

*English language edition, except USA and Canada,*
*published by*
Associated Business Programmes Ltd
17 Buckingham Gate, London SW1

*Published in the USA and Canada by*
Halsted Press, a Division of
John Wiley & Sons Inc
New York

First published 1975

This book has been printed in Great Britain
by The Anchor Press Ltd & bound by
Wm Brendon and Son Ltd, both of Tiptree, Essex

ISBN 0 85227 030 5

To Frances

# Contents

Markets – Alternative Exporting Methods – Promotion Overseas – Summary of the Critical Factors for Success in Exporting – Checklist

Richard Skinner

Marketing Functions – Marketing Personnel – Keeping Staff to a Minimum – Selecting the Team – Control – Securing Acceptance of the Marketing Function – The Rewards of Marketing – Checklist

David Jones

MARKETING is all those activities concerned with purchases and sales of goods and services in industrial, commercial, institutional and consumer markets and between organisational buyers and sellers.

AUBREY WILSON

MARKETING is concerned with all the exhilarating big things and all the troublesome little things that must be done in every nook and cranny of the entire organisation in order to achieve the corporate purpose of attracting and holding customers.

THEODORE LEVITT

# Preface

Marketing is widely associated with large budgets. In many firms sales activity is deemed an essential counterpart to production, but marketing a luxury which cannot always be afforded, particularly in times of recession and restricted cash flow. Many of the individual marketing functions are thought of as being inevitably high cost. This is largely due to the well-publicised and heavy expenditures laid out by producers of consumer goods on such functions as advertising, market research and public relations. The most cursory examination of the reality of marketing shows that such thinking is erroneous. While many situations do call for high-cost marketing, which can be justified in terms of the resultant financial benefits, large budgets are not an inevitable sequel to a firm embracing the marketing concept. Certainly marketing expenditure will be higher than that incurred by a sales department but this should be more than compensated by the additional benefits.

It is probably better to do nothing than to market badly or inadequately, but many companies fail to realise that a limited marketing budget well-spent can not only add substanitally to the profit yield from their productive assets but will also place them in a position to benefit from future market opportunities. By turning a blind eye to such skills as product development, advertising, public relations and market research, in the belief that they are too expensive, companies wilfully increase the already enormous risks inherent in the modern business environment.

The purpose of this book is to show how firms with limited funds available can still take advantage of modern marketing theory and practice. A secondary objective will be to show how to optimise the yield from any given budget allocation. Thus the content should be of interest to all firms, large and small, engaging, or about to engage, in marketing activity.

The idea for the book arose out of the almost casual observation that although there are many books on the principles of marketing and even on the detailed application of marketing techniques, few, if any, discuss in detail the cost of the marketing function. Having absorbed the theory, therefore, students of marketing are thrown out into a hard world where budgets count for everything and fine theories for very little. The same applies to businessmen coming fresh to marketing, whose early skirmishes with research, product launches, advertising, public relations and sales campaigns normally serve only to convince them that these are expensive techniques indeed. Nor does the image of marketing do much to dispel the impression that firms lacking limitless resources would be best advised to forget it and concentrate on sales. Marketing men have a reputation for extravagance and who can deny, looking at certain marketing activities, that this reputation is not, in some cases, justified.

Marketing has often developed so rapidly within companies that too much attention has been paid to the development of the techniques and too little to the achievement of value for money. All too many marketing men have sought the spectacular at the expense of the effective. Elaborate promotion techniques, extravagant advertising and exotic conferences appear the norm rather than the exception. Given the primary function of marketing (the attraction and maintenance of customers) and the basic tendency in human nature for the novel to become commonplace, perhaps it is to be expected that marketing would in time become increasingly exotic and expensive. But that does not mean that *all* marketing is *necessarily* expensive or that some of the large sums of money that are inevitably required cannot be justified in terms of the rewards they bring. Beneath the fanfares and public demonstrations of opulence, a large number of firms have succeeded in embracing the marketing concept and have successfully implemented it without incurring heady expenditures either beyond their means or out of proportion with the benefits they have obtained. These firms have built up a body of experience on how to minimise their marketing expenditure. They know when large budgets are justified, and they also know of the battery of short cuts and cost-saving techniques which can minimise the wastage in marketing expenditure. As an activity, marketing is itself concerned with the minimisation of wastage caused by inadequate knowledge of customers' requirements, poor or inappropriate product development or deficiencies in the flow of information about the product to the customer. Thus marketing people should be sensitive to the effects of wastage in their own activities.

This book is, therefore, not only about how to market on a small budget, but also how to minimise the budget required for any given marketing function. To write exclusively for the small firm would not be to make the best of our material; after all there are greater savings to be made in those firms misapplying large budgets. We could also have run into serious problems of definition, for how small is a small budget? While the absolute sums are obviously important marketing budgets are only meaningful when related to the scale of the task being undertaken. Thus what is small in one context may be ludicrously expensive in another. We have, therefore, attempted to concentrate on the techniques of budget minimisation rather than state the absolute amounts which should be considered in given circumstances, as these would in any event soon be out-of-date.

To write on such a subject requires an intimate knowledge of marketing practices and the benefit of long experience struggling with inadequate budgets. I have been fortunate to work with a team of contributors who not only have survived this experience but have been able to document their experiences lucidly. To put their budget-saving recommendations into perspective, each of the contributors has described the objectives of the function they are discussing. Thus, although we did not set out to write yet another introduction to marketing, that is inevitably a component of the text.

We have also tried to avoid writing exclusively about either industrial or consumer marketing. It was felt that the lessons were common to both types of marketing even if the scale of the budgets in consumer marketing were normally substantially higher than those in the industrial world. As can be seen from the biographies, the contributors come from both sides of the fence – some with experience that is exclusively consumer-orientated, and others with experience that is exclusively industiral. All, however, have taken the trouble to examine the problem from both standpoints wherever there are significant differences. As with previous authors of marketing texts, none of the contributors had specifically considered the problem of marketing on a *small* budget before and some at first felt that it could not be done. The reader will be able to judge how well they have applied themselves to the task, and how rich is the experience they have passed on.

The chapter headings reflect the major marketing functions and as far as possible the normal division of labour within marketing departments. This approach not only provided each of the contributors with a more manageable task but also facilitates the use of the book. The chapters are self-contained and the book may be dipped into by those wishing to refer to only part of the subject at any one time. As a result, however, there are a number of recurrent themes since many of the cost-saving techniques may be applied to several functions.

The editor of any book learns much from his contributors; indeed that is one of the principal reasons for undertaking what can be a demanding task. For that I am indebted to all of them, but I am particularly grateful to Mark Sloan, Norman Hart and John Naylor, whose suggestions for further contributors were very gratefully received. My biggest debt, however, is to Aubrey Wilson, who not only provided the original idea but has also been a constant source of encouragement and inspiration throughout the preparation of the text. My thanks are also due to all my other colleagues at Industrial Market Research and Associated Business Programmes, and particularly to Jenny Kelly, who managed to keep pace with the mountains of paperwork that an edited book invariably produces.

*London 1975* CHRISTOPHER WEST

# The Contributors: Biographical Notes

CHRISTOPHER J. WEST, B.Sc.Econ., the editor of this book, is a graduate of the London School of Economics. Prior to joining the Board of Industrial Market Research Ltd., where he is now deputy managing director, Mr. West was engaged on economic research and planning for a major international petro-chemical firm and subsequently served as a consulting economist with Eurofinance, a Paris-based financial organisation. In this capacity he carried out numerous European-wide industry studies and macro-economic forecasts for leading Continental and American banks, as well as specialised studies for the European Economic Community and the Organisation for Economic Co-operation and Development.

GORDON T. BRAND, B.Sc.Econ., is a consultant and principal lecturer in Marketing at the South West Regional Management Centre at Bristol Polytechnic. Before taking up his appointment at Bristol he was head of research at Industrial Market Research Ltd. He began his career as a salesman in the Consumer Products Division of ITT and later transferred to the Components Group where he established and operated a marketing research department. In 1968 he was awarded a fellowship tenable at the Harvard Graduate Business School by the Foundation for Management Education. Gordon Brand is the author of *The Industrial Buying Decision*. Currently he is extending his research into the implications for marketing management of industrial purchasing procedures to the newly formed local authority areas.

RICHARD W. F. EASSIE is a marketing consultant specialising in new product development. He is a director of Kraushar Andrews & Eassie Ltd. and of Pricing Research Ltd. Previously, he was a brand manager with Beechams, marketing manager of John Haddon & Co. and a director of D & F Marketing Development Ltd. Richard Eassie is also editor of *Mintel* and author of *New Products in Grocers, 1974*, and writes and broadcasts frequently on marketing topics.

BRIAN P. FLETCHER, B.A., is the deputy chairman of Associated Sprayers Ltd. He began his business career as a marketing assistant with Proctor & Gamble, then joined General Foods in 1963. During his ten years with them, he occupied a variety of positions in marketing and development, spending his last two years as development director in charge of corporate planning, acquisitions, new business ventures and R & D.

NORMAN HART was appointed director of the CAM Foundation in 1972 having previously been chief marketing executive of IAB Marketing, a Government-sponsored management consultancy. Starting as a student in electrical engineering, he became a technical salesman, and then moved into sales management. He joined an advertising agency, Roles & Parker Ltd., on the account-service side, and was group chief executive when he left to join a Unilever company, Thames Board Mills, as publicity manager. He subsequently became marketing manager, and finally went into publishing with Morgan Grampian where he was divisional general manager. Mr. Hart is the author of *Industrial Publicity* and, as well as writing regularly for the management and marketing press, is preparing a new textbook on marketing terms. He is also a frequent lecturer, both in the UK and overseas, on advertising effectiveness, public relations, marketing and industrial communications.

SIMON C. HODGSON, M.A., is marketing director of Kenrick & Jefferson Ltd., printers to the computer industry. After five years with Shell International as a student and graduate engineer he joined Industrial Market Research Ltd. where he was engaged on a wide variety of market and industry research projects within the UK and overseas. His overseas research experience covers countries such as Germany, France, Spain, Italy, the United States and Canada, as well as a number of the smaller industrialised countries. He is currently responsible for home and overseas marketing of specialised stationery for the computer industry, as well as a range of consumer print and promotional product publishing.

DAVID JONES is surveys editor of the *Investors' Chronicle*. After national service (where he was commissioned in the Worcestershire Regiment) and Oxford (where he read Ancient History and Philosophy) he joined United Steel Company as a graduate trainee. Following a period in the group's commercial research department at Sheffield he joined Alcan's market research department. For two years he was a research consultant with the Economist Intelligence Unit in London. In march 1967 he joined *The Times* as a member of the original team which launched the paper's Business News section. During the six years with *The Times* he covered many aspects of industrial and consumer marketing. In addition to his work as a financial journalist, he writes articles for *History Today*, book reviews for *The Times* and history books for children.

JOHN NAYLOR trained in electrical engineering with AEI, became a technical writer there, progressing later to the management side in the home and overseas publicity departments. He then moved to Morgan Grampian (Publishers) as marketing development manager of their IEA division where he worked on a number of leading technical journals. In 1969 he joined Dymo Ltd., specialising in visual communications. Starting as UK Advertising Manager, he later became marketing planning manager and is now resident in Belgium as label systems product manager for Europe, Africa and the Near East.

RICHARD N. SKINNER, B.A., acquired his marketing experience in the office equipment and communications industries. He joined Reliance Systems Ltd., a subsidiary of the General Electric Company, as sales manager in 1964. His work since then has included the planning and implementation of a major diversification programme and the expansion and reorganisation of the sales force to its present strength of 150. In 1971 he was appointed marketing director. He is the author of *Launching New Products in Competitive Markets*, a study of the marketing techniques applicable to new products.

MARK SLOAN, B.Sc.Econ. is marketing director for General Foods Scandinavia, responsible for the marketing and development functions, in the company's operations across the four Scandinavian countries. Previous assignments with the General Foods UK company include the function of coffee development manager, in which he initiated, developed and launched Bird's Mellow Coffee, and the position of business studies manager, in which he negotiated the licensing arrangements, and set up the manufacturing and selling organisation, for the company's vending venture. Before joining General Foods, Mark Sloan was with Unilever, and Ogilvy, Benson & Mather.

CHAPTER 1

# The Cost of the Marketing Function

By Christopher West

In 1970, British manufacturing industry spent approximately 10 per cent
of its sales revenue on various marketing activities. This covered the wages
and salaries of marketing and sales personnel, the cost of packaging,
advertising, promotion, point-of-sale material, market research, transport
and distribution and such sundry operating expenses as postage, telephone
calls and telex messages. Not surprisingly, since marketing is by its nature
a labour-intensive activity, wages and salaries accounted for the largest
proportion of the marketing bill although packaging and transportation
were also major cost items, between them absorbing 47 per cent of marketing expenditure. Beside these figures the sums spent on market research
and publicity material look very small indeed, and even advertising
expenditure, equated with marketing in many people's minds, amounted
to only a third of the wages component.

FIGURE 1.1.

*Marketing Expenditure by British*
*Manufacturing Industry – 1970[1]*

|  | £ million | Per cent |
|---|---|---|
| Wages and salaries of sales and marketing | 1,300 | 35·8 |
| Media advertising | 450 | 12·4 |
| Publicity and point-of-sale material | 100 | 2·8 |
| Market research | 20 | 0·6 |
| Packaging | 900 | 24·8 |
| Transport and distribution | 800 | 22·0 |
| Miscellaneous charges (including postage, telephone and telex) | 60 | 1·6 |
| TOTAL MARKETING | 3,630 | 100·0 |
| % SALES REVENUE | 9·5 | |
| % VALUE ADDED | 24·0 | |

[1]Figures are author's estimates based on a variety of sources.

Marketing expenditure varies significantly within industry. In general, firms selling directly to the consumer, which tend to have a heavy commitment to packaging and advertising, spend significantly more on marketing than firms selling exclusively into industrial markets. Thus food, drink and tobacco companies spend an average 14 per cent of their sales revenue on marketing while shipbuilders spend only 5 per cent.

FIGURE 1.2.

*Estimated Marketing Expenditure*
*by Industry Sector*

|  | Per cent Sales Revenue |
|---|---|
| Food, drink and tobacco | 14·0 |
| Chemicals and allied | 13·0 |
| metal manufacturing | 5·0 |
| Engineering and electrical goods | 10·0 |
| Shipbuilding and marine engineering | 5·0 |
| Vehicles | 6·5 |
| Metal goods n.e.s. | 6·0 |
| Textiles | 5·0 |
| Leather, leather goods and fur | 5·0 |
| Clothing and footwear | 7·0 |
| Bricks, pottery, glass, cement, etc. | 14·0 |
| Timber and furniture | 8·0 |
| Paper, printing and publishing | 9·5 |
| Other manufacturing industry | 9·0 |
| TOTAL MANUFACTURING INDUSTRY | 9·5 |

Comparable data for individual firms are only rarely available, though it is evident that marketing practices do vary considerably between organisations. The scale and nature of a firm's marketing effort can be so vital to its success in the market place, that, not surprisingly, management will seek to limit the outflow of information on the subject. Of course, some marketing activity by its very nature is highly visible, and it is possible to compute individual firms' expenditure on such items as advertising and specific research projects. This, however, is barely representative of total marketing expenditure and is more likely to mislead than to illuminate.

The size of the marketing budget tends to increase with the size of the firm but an examination of the marketing practices of a number of organisations of all sizes operating in a broad spectrum of activities shows that the relationship is not as clear cut as might at first be assumed. Many large firms have surprisingly small marketing budgets while many small firms, being almost exclusively marketing operations, spend large sums on marketing. To some extent these variations can be explained by the activities in which the firms are engaging and the extent to which they have embraced the marketing concept, but there are other forces at work. The principal reasons for which an individual marketing budget may be restricted may be summarised as follows:

- The level of sales and future growth expectations may not warrant an extensive marketing effort.
- The firm may have an undeveloped, or underdeveloped, marketing function.
- The firm may be operating in a market which does not call for an extensive marketing effort.
- Management may have decided to adopt a minimum investment policy and therefore restrict the flow of funds until the success of the venture can be demonstrated.
- The firm may be suffering from cash starvation, in which case marketing expenditure is the easiest cost item to cut back on.

All these symptoms are equally likely to be present in large and small organisations.

The size of the marketing budget in money terms is a less significant measure than the proportion of sales revenue which is devoted to marketing activity. On this basis there is virtually no correlation between marketing expenditure and the size of the firm. The implication of this is that firms developing marketing budgets have little in the way of hard and fast rules to follow and must revert to first principles, or their own or their competitors' track record for guidance. The problem is exacerbated for those with only a small budget available by the fact that they are unlikely to have the resources to try everything. The problem can be resolved by *understanding* the nature and purpose of marketing activity and the minimum resources acceptable in any given marketing situation. Once this has been achieved careful *planning* of marketing activity should ensure that wasted activity is minimised, and *monitoring* will show whether the planned activities were effective, thereby providing new inputs to the next budgeting procedure.

## Composition of the Marketing Budget

Total marketing expenditure is closely related to the number and type of functions which are included within the orbit of the marketing department. In its broadest sense, marketing relates to the organisation and performance of those business activities that facilitate the exchange of goods and services between maker and user.[1] In addition, marketing is deeply concerned with the future survival of the company and should, therefore, include a strong forward-looking component in its activities.

[1]Leslie Rodger, *Marketing in a Competitive Economy*, Associated Business Programmes (London, 1973), p. 21.

Thus planning future products in the light of customers' known or presumed requirements is an essential counterbalance to the inevitable preoccupation with current sales. The full spectrum of marketing activity includes the following: product planning, research and development, test marketing, market research, public relations, advertising, promotion, pricing, sales, merchandising and physical distribution.

Those marketing on a small budget may well engage in all of the above activities at some time or other but not necessarily on a continuous basis. The first response to budgetary constraint is to be selective in the marketing techniques that are employed. To do this effectively requires careful planning and a deep understanding of what the market will accept.

**Marketing Inputs**

In contrast to many production operations, marketing activity is largely dependent on people. Mechanisation has facilitated some of the marketing tasks but has not significantly reduced the demand for marketing personnel. Furthermore, physical distribution apart, few marketing posts can be filled by untrained or manual labour. The nature of the work demands intelligence and creative talents. It follows, therefore, that the *per capita* salary bill in the marketing department may be significantly higher than that experienced elsewhere in the organisation. The small budget marketer must, therefore, ensure an efficient utilisation of the staff at his disposal. This may be achieved either by doubling up on job functions or by calling in outside specialists as and when required.[1] The use of consultants for certain marketing functions is a recurring topic throughout the following chapters of this book.

**Planning the Marketing Budget**

The control of marketing expenditure, or to put it another way, the maximisation of benefits from any given level of expenditure, demands careful planning. The two major components of the plan are a detailed statement of what is to be achieved during the planning period, and a translation of that statement into its budgetary (financial) implications. The result is a marketing budget related to a course of action to be taken by the firm. The statement of objectives should include:

● Sales and profit forecasts.
● Specific marketing targets, such as the penetration of new market sectors, concentration of effort on certain customer types, geographical extension of marketing activity.
● New product developments and their contribution to turnover and profit.

To create the budget the objectives must then be converted into specific

[1]See chapter 10 ('Organising for Marketing on a Small Budget').

courses of action drawn from the armoury of marketing techniques. It is at this stage that the level of marketing expenditure will become apparent and that steps to contain expenditure should be taken. The firm with sizeable marketing objectives will need to support them with an adequate marketing budget, and if the budget is to be trimmed then so should the objectives.

The choice of marketing techniques is itself dependent on the requirements of the market being served and the firm's own judgement on how these can best be met within the budget available. There is no single correct solution to this problem; different strategies may well provide comparable results and competitive reaction may well frustrate what would otherwise prove a suitable approach. There is also scope for economy of action. It is no more essential to apply every conceivable marketing technique in order to market a product or service effectively than it is to use every type of machine tool to produce an engineered component. Just as presses, drills, honers and lathes have their specific (and often overlapping) applications in a workshop, so do market research, advertising, public relations and direct mail in the marketing of the finished output. This message is of particular importance to firms operating on a limited marketing budget. A selective and finely balanced marketing strategy is not only more effective but also less costly than an all-embracing marketing programme. It does, however, place a premium on careful market planning and accurate knowledge not only of market requirements but also the most effective means of communicating with and reaching the ultimate customer.

When planning the deployment of a small budget it is necessary to distinguish between essential and peripheral marketing activities. The latter are functions which may be useful in supporting the major marketing activity but can be dropped without seriously affecting the sales yield in the short term. The designation of each type of marketing activity will depend on the specific marketing problem being faced and the nature of the marketing environment. Advertising and public relations may be essential activities for a firm attempting to build an image in a new market but a luxury for a monopoly supplier in a well-established market. Personal selling may be essential when the sales programme demands a high level of customer education on the value of the product and the credibility of the firm as a supplier, but may be wasteful when the value of each order is low and direct mail is an acceptable method of reaching customers and receiving orders. Each marketing situation should be carefully assessed and the minimum acceptable approach decided on. Depth market information is a key input to this procedure, which implies that market research as well as market planning are invariably essential components of a marketing programme.

## Setting the Budget

In all business functions expenditure is studied on two levels; the amounts which are budgeted, that is, forecasts of expenditure to achieve given objectives, and the amounts which are actually spent. Accepting that there are many firms, particularly small firms, which do not undertake annual forward budgeting procedures, in all other organisations the difference between budgeted and actual expenditure is one key measure of the efficiency of management. If no budgets are set then the control of expenditure is at best haphazard. This, of course, applies to all corporate activities, not only marketing, and it is important that the marketing budget is integrated with the production and other budgets to ensure that they are pulling in the same direction. There is little point in having an undernourished marketing function and a replete production department, only to find that the marketing effort is inadequate for the task of selling the volume of goods produced, and vice versa.

Those setting marketing budgets are faced with two alternative approaches. They may either set a total budget which is allocated between the various functions (top down) or they can build up to a total from the separate budgets developed for each function (bottom up). Each approach has its merits and demerits in terms of the effect that it has on the size of the overall budget. It can be argued that greater fragmentation of budget setting implied in the bottom up approach, tends to escalate the budget since individual components of marketing activity are more closely scrutinised and a stronger case made for spending more money. When working to a fixed budget allocation, as is achieved by the top down approach, managers are likely to give more thought to the cost effectiveness of their programmes and the cost savings which can be achieved. There is a danger, however, that top down budgeting will choke expenditure to the point that it is insufficient to achieve the objectives of the marketing programme. The resolution of this problem may be achieved by discussion among those responsible for the implementation of the marketing programme, which in small organisations is not likely to be a time-consuming operation.

In setting a marketing budget a key problem is the lack of any hard and fast relationship between money spent and the results achieved. Unlike production where an investment in capital plant will produce a calculable effect on the volume, nature or efficiency of output, the effects of marketing expenditure are known only by monitoring. Even this can provide only a guide for there is no guarantee that the market will continually respond in an identical manner to specific marketing inputs. Organisations setting a budget for the first time lack precedent for a guide and must rely on a more fundamental approach, namely a continual recycling of objectives, techniques and costs until a satisfactory balance of what needs to be achieved and what can be afforded, is attained. It is also advisable to keep the progress of the marketing programme under constant review so that experience can be fed back continually into the budgeting process.

## Assessing the Budget

By focusing on the *cost* of the marketing function, this book is in danger of reinforcing, if not engendering, the dangerous tendency among firms to regard cost as the only criterion by which to evaluate their marketing programmes. 'We'll do it if we can afford it' is a common enough sentiment when appraising specific marketing proposals, when in many situations firms should be asking 'Can we afford *not* to do it?' Marketing costs must be related to the benefits which can accrue from the expenditure and providing the cost/benefit equation is favourable then the expenditure may be considered worthwhile. Furthermore, much marketing effort is a long-term investment in that it establishes a company's reputation and image in the market place and generates new products which will sustain the company's future business. Therefore, in evaluating the benefits a long-term view should be taken.

The preoccupation with cost at the expense of benefits is not difficult to explain. Costs are easily computed and are virtually certain to be incurred once a programme is committed, regardless of conditions in the marketing environment. Benefits, on the other hand, cannot be demonstrated with certainty, often cannot be quantified and may evaporate if trading conditions deteriorate. In addition, as stated above, benefits can rarely be attributed to any specific injection of marketing funds. Much marketing expenditure is therefore an act of faith, or even a defence mechanism, since the only way to prove its value is to stop doing it and see what happens. Of course, as later chapters will show, there are methods of demonstrating the probable effects of marketing expenditure, but many will argue cynically that these merely represent yet more ways of separating the unwilling marketer from his cash.

## Monitoring the Marketing Budget

No marketing plan can be regarded as complete unless an effective monitoring system is incorporated within the programme of activities. Certainly the small budget marketer needs to know what he has actually spent and (insofar as possible) the effects of his expenditure in improving the profit yield from his activities, if he is to be in a position to judge whether the effort has been worthwhile and correctly oriented. No marketing decisions can be taken in the light of perfect knowledge of the market environment, but practical experience can only be a substitute if monitoring takes place.

A constant review of marketing progress in relation to the money expended serves another important purpose. It enables senior management to vet the performance of marketing personnel. The latter tend by nature to be incurable optimists which, if unfettered, can let their enthusiasm run away with them. Being held closely to account for their actions is an uncomfortable process but is nevertheless effective in curbing excesses.

Budgeting periods tend to be of a year or six months yet in many markets the effects of expenditure can be seen well before that time period is up. Though expensive on time there is no reason why monitoring should not be carried out on a monthly basis. The 'pay-off' will occur whenever monitoring enables management to make budget-saving changes of course in mid-period.

The monitoring process should examine the actual flow of funds into marketing activity and should concentrate on an examination of any deviations from planned expenditure. The explanations for unscheduled expenditure can often be more revealing than the effects of budgeted items. The implementation of a marketing budget highlights all the problems and side effects which cannot be anticipated when the budget is being set, and it is important to capture this experience if the same mistakes are not to be made twice. It is important also to monitor the changes that occur in the market place itself during the period that the budget is being implemented. These may reinforce or offset the effects of the company's strategy and themselves account for a success or a failure in marketing effort. These effects must be discounted if a true evaluation of the marketing programme is to be made.

To monitor its efforts effectively a company must be aware of the position from which it is starting. Thus some form of benchmark study should be completed before the effort takes place showing the market position, image and reputation of the company and the present size and structure of the market it is serving. It is the rolling forward of this information that shows the degree of success, or otherwise, that the company is achieving. The activities of competitive suppliers should be included in the monitoring process. It is important to know what they are up to and how they react to a marketing initiative. It is said that imitation is the sincerest form of flattery and this is as true in business as in any other field. When competitors copy a marketing tactic there is a strong chance that they have felt its effectiveness.

Monitoring can be carried out at several points within the company's organisation. Recording expenditures can be carried out by the accounts department and fed on a regular basis to management. Salesmen's reports can be tailored to provide a subjective market eye-view. More objective information should be forthcoming from specially commissioned market research reports and the competitors' response may be picked up at trade association meetings or by discussions with customers themselves.

Revolutions are comparatively rare in marketing. Evolution is the norm as the effects of marketing activity build up over a period of years.

New expenditure tends to alter directions rather than cause fundamental change which means that monitoring activity must be fairly finely tuned in order to be effective. Firms spending small budgets will tend to have less momentous impacts on the market place than their high-spending colleagues and must therefore be more patient when evaluating their effectiveness.

The chapters which follow examine each of the key marketing functions to show their individual roles in the marketing process and the means by which expenditure on each of them can be minimised. As experts in their respective subjects each of the contributors has assumed that no marketing programme is complete unless his particular activity is included. As the sentient reader will by now be aware, this is not necessarily the case, but by reading the chapters he will be able to judge how useful the activities are.

## CHECKLIST

- What is the company's total expenditure on marketing activities?

- How is this distributed between the various marketing functions?

- Who decides on the level and type of marketing expenditure?

- Are marketing budgets prepared and if so by whom?

- Is marketing expenditure compared with amounts spent by competitive or similar companies?

- What personnel are available for marketing within the organisation?

- Have lists of appropriate consultants been compiled and vetted?

- What formal review procedures are there for examining the progress of the marketing campaign?

- Are management accounts presented in such a way that marketing expenditure can readily be identified?

CHAPTER 2

# Product Planning and the Search for New Products on a Small Budget

By Mark Sloan

It is widely believed that major industrial and commercial achievements stem only from the ability to command and direct vast resources. Certainly this is true in many instances – space-shots, hovertrains, computers and perhaps less grandiosely now, motor cars, instant coffee, and substitutes for meat and dairy products. But, in fact, much of what we see represents skilful and large-scale *exploitation* of a basic idea or technique that had its origin in much less awe-inspiring surroundings. The work of such people as Edison, John Logie Baird or Barnes Wallis was not conducted on an infinite budget.

The object of such analogies is to point out that a large budget is not necessarily a prerequisite for successful product development, although it may well be for optimum exploitation. Equally, though, it must be admitted that the area of what might be called 'technologically fed' innovation (probably most compellingly illustrated by computer development) is growing rapidly, and requires enormous resources and investment as the minimum starting price.

However, in the great majority of areas where the smaller company is active a large development budget, whilst reassuring, may not only be unnecessary but may also be disruptive in that it encourages waste, too wide a programme and detracts from the single-minded approach necessary for successful innovation.

A small budget leaves little room for error and so demands concentration on realistic and practical development objectives, rather than 'blue skies' projects. The proportionate investment made by the smaller company in development work is usually much greater than that of the large corporation, and this necessitates a ruthless adherence to systems and guidelines to ensure, as far as possible, maximum value for every development penny spent.

This chapter will therefore commence with the question 'Are you sure you want new products?' not only to provoke thought on what a development programme really entails, but also to demonstrate that there may be avenues in the existing business which are better investment returners. This first section also highlights the importance of an integrated planning approach to the business as a necessary initial step in the attempt to improve profitability.

Subsequent sections explore ways of systematically reviewing the areas of new product search, understanding of the stages of development, financial criteria and controls, and some suggestions for ways of getting the job done and avoiding the pitfalls of unnecessary wastage.

**Are you sure you want New Products?**

Ultimately there can be only one reason for wanting new products: to improve profitability. This is the overall objective and there are many ways of achieving it; new product development is only one strategy that could be employed, acquisition, merger, venture development, franchising and licensing all being viable alternatives, particularly if increased exploitation of existing products or processes represents the real opportunity. This concept of innovation versus further exploitation is a key one in the initial thinking on development, and will be referred to again later.

**Taking stock of the company**

The starting point for evaluating whether or not a new products programme should be initiated, or continued, is a complete inventory of the company. This is essentially an audit of what the company is, its present status and how it got there. The information for such an audit probably already exists, but perhaps in an unco-ordinated way, with each company manager having his own slightly different conception of the company. For the smaller company, pulling this information together and keeping it updated as necessary, represents an investment in a senior man's time – ranging from a few weeks to a few months, depending on company size and complexity. For the large corporation, such an audit would require a much more significant investment, possibly leading to the establishment of a department for corporate planning.

This company inventory or audit should attempt to detail the following:

● The company's financial status and performance history.

● The business environment and trends, with their relevance to the company's present and future situation.

● The company's strengths and weaknesses, e.g. in terms of access to capital, management, distribution, sites, product portfolio, production facilities and technologies.

To be effective, this company audit should be as objective as possible, and be updated regularly. Such an assessment of the business can then be fed into an integrated planning process, the level of sophistication of which will depend on the company's requirements (an indication of the steps involved is given in Figure 2.1.).

From this starting point, a systematic assessment of the development of the existing business can be made. Similarly, management needs to evolve realistic objectives for the business at some future point (say, over three to five years), specified in target terms, e.g. turnover, return on funds employed (ROFE), return on investment (ROI), earnings per share, contribution profit or profit before tax (PBT). Comparison of the projections for the existing business and the future position required will identify the gap to be filled with additional activity. Only at this stage, when such an assessment has been made on the scale of activity required to meet the objectives set, can judgements begin to be made concerning the optimum way of arriving at them. The potential costs, risks and possible pay-off of a new products programme, from a decision to innovate, can be set alongside comparable judgements on a decision to further exploit existing properties within the company.

**Innovation versus exploitation**

The transition between innovation and exploitation can be seen clearly from the well-known matrix of products and markets, new and existing. In descending order of difficulty, the four possibilities are as follows:

● New products in new markets.

● New products in existing markets.

● Existing products in new markets.

● Existing products in existing markets.

It is often thought that this order also represents a descending scale of potential returns, and many instances could be cited which would seem to substantiate the thought. However, the Bofors company in Sweden, an old-established armaments business, branched out into the toothpaste market on the back of a discovery in its laboratories of a process which substantially reduced the abrasive effect of existing products on teeth. This was heralded as a most welcome diversification, and was probably seen as the forerunner of a whole series of new products in new markets which would broaden the company's base and reduce its dependence on armaments. After a detailed company evaluation following a change of management it was realised that such projects were sapping the company's strengths, were taking the company into areas where it had no expertise and most important, were distracting attention from effectively developing the current business in which, it was discovered, substantial opportunities

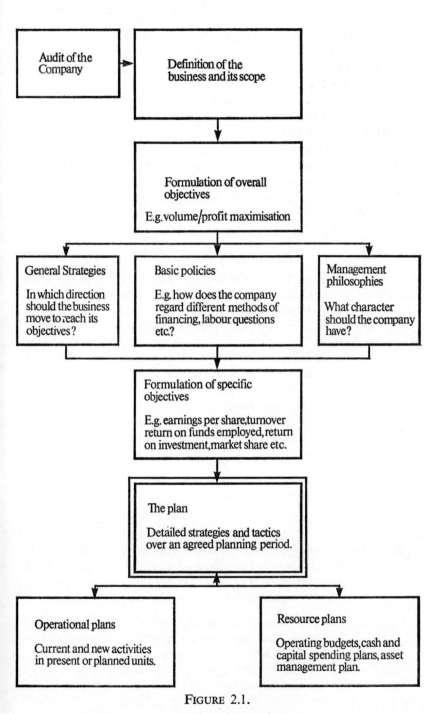

FIGURE 2.1.

*Steps in the Planning Process*

existed. The concept of new products in new markets is an exciting and challenging one, but the risks attached in setting this as a company objective, and the dangers attendant in operating in unfamiliar markets, should not be under-rated.

In practice, most companies consciously attempt to keep at least one of the variables constant so that their planned innovation is either in new products for markets with which they are familiar and have knowledge or 'feel' (which this chapter goes on to discuss), or in deploying existing products, the characteristics of which they know intimately, into unfamiliar markets, for example by setting up an export department. Very few small companies would consciously plan to develop new products for new markets; even large companies rely on acquisition for obtaining the necessary expertise for such diversification, as practised by cigarette companies across the world. Alternatively companies that stumble across or spin-off an innovation applicable to fields completely divorced from their existing business, can explore the possibilities of patent rights and then either license or franchise, or possibly enter into a joint venture with a partner who has knowledge of the field.

The exploitation of existing products in existing markets is a route that surprisingly, although on the doorstep, is not fully explored by many companies. Gillette initially did not exploit its stainless steel blade technology in the United Kingdom and allowed Wilkinson Sword a clear lead for many years, a lead which proved very expensive to close. For the smaller company it obviously makes sense to fully round out the existing business, not only because this is the easiest and least risky way of improving profitability, but also because any substantial gaps by-passed in the existing business can be filled by a competitor striking at the heart of today's profits.

## Ways of looking at the existing business

There is always an attraction in the novel, which transcends the relative dullness of the familiar. But the existing business is a 'bird in the hand' and its fixed costs are already being covered. The greater part of any improvement in contribution towards these fixed costs should fall through to the profit line on the profit and loss account. The following are some instances of ways in which the current business can be continuously evaluated.

*Product quality* – This might be improved to command a higher price and/or greater customer loyalty. Conversely, the product could be over-engineered in such areas as formulation, types of raw material and packaging. Carefully monitored reductions in the direct cost of goods may not affect in any way the customer's perception of the product.

*Positioning and image* – Something as simple as changing the content or tone of brand communication through packaging, media and distribution sites, can substantially improve a brand's sales and profitability. Care must, of course, be taken not to compromise the expectations of the existing franchise, but there are ways of segmenting communication. Johnson's for example, were aware for some years of the adult usage of their baby powder product. By skilfully riding with this usage, positioning it as a natural extension to baby usage ('Are you still a Johnson's baby')? and communicating it via different media – television and magazines – they were able to increase sales. Similarly, the Cheeseborough-Pond's product, Vaseline, was expanded into nursery usage and its image fashioned accordingly by the expedient of packing part of the production into plastic jars decorated with a nursery motif.

*Performance improvements* – Knowing how and why a particular product is used can often suggest inexpensive ways in which its performance can be improved, and as a concomitant, its sales and profitability. For example, the new 'softer' margarines take into account the problems of spreading straight from the refrigerator, salt packets often contain an integral plastic pourer and Dot lavatory powder is packaged to provide a 'puffing' facility.

Each of these ways of evaluating the existing business can improve sales and profits by expanding the franchise or encouraging existing users to buy more. Additionally, two further areas can be looked at:

*Value analysis* – The technique of dissecting and analysing every element of the product, from types of raw material used to the size of labels, the amount of adhesive and the number of staples in the fibre-case, to see how far each of the elements contributes to the whole, and in which areas savings can be made.

*Distribution/trade support* – If a product is not available, because either it is not stocked or it is out of stock, the customer cannot buy it. Time, effort and possibly also money spent in maximising availability can be expected to bring immediate returns, as well as ensuring maximum return from all other promotional activities.

A recent study by the Nielsen company on the use of coupons by grocery companies showed that consumers redeeming their coupons were faced with up to two in five shops who were out of stock when they wanted to buy. New distribution channels are also good investment returners: the vending industry has been actively exploiting distribution possibilities for many years. Changes in life-style also open up new purchasing channels. For example, the increase in car travel, in terms of both the number of cars and passenger miles travelled, has led to the marked and growing importance of petrol stations as purveyors of everything from groceries through confectionery to cassettes.

Similarly, brand extension opportunities (that is, pack, size, flavour changes, etc.) should consistently be reviewed. These provide immediate synergy in the key areas of purchasing, production and sales-force time. The risks are usually reduced, firstly, because the scale is smaller and second, because the line extension trades off the established franchise of its parent and, therefore, requires less marketing investment.

The marketing policy for Cadbury's chocolate block lines for the last few years appears to have been one of constant extension from the Dairy Milk base. Old Jamaica, Ice Breaker and Country Style, whilst appearing to be new products, all share the same basic materials and have similar moulding and packing lines, wrapping requirements and bulk packaging. Similarly, Bird's Trifle has vastly increased its business by the addition of other flavours to the originally launched variety. In the case of industrial products there are equally abundant opportunities for the development of new variations on existing products. It is also possible to locate new market sectors and applications hitherto unexploited yet offering rewarding potential, for an unmodified or only slightly altered product. The offshore oil search in the North Sea represents just such an opportunity for a host of industrial companies.

However, for the line-extension route to be successful, it is vital to have a clear idea of the amount of business that will be taken from the parent product, and from this to ensure that the product's profitability is not diluted by conversion to a lower average margin.

### Refining the Areas of Search for New Products

If, after objectively evaluating the business and identifying and assigning a value to a desired future position, it appears that a gap exists which cannot be filled by rounding out the current business or placing existing products into new markets, then it is appropriate to consider developing new products. But, as we have seen, it is unlikely that any company is consciously going to develop new products and then look for a market for them. A few of the very largest corporations do have 'think tanks' or 'blue skies groups', but where they exist they reflect the companies' position in the very forefront of their fields requiring some level of breakthrough thinking, and is only of academic interest to the smaller company whose work must, to a greater or lesser degree, be adaptive. Consequently, new product development work starts by identifying areas of interest – markets that can then be looked at in detail for opportunities. But if the name of the game is new products in existing markets, how do we define existing markets?

Ever since Theodore Levitt described marketing myopia,[1] that is, too
<hr>
[1]Theodore Levitt, *Innovation in Marketing*, Pan Books London, 1968).

narrow a definition of the field within which a company is or should be operating, it has become extremely important not to slavishly follow conventional wisdom in defining 'existing markets'. Above a certain level, of course, the definition is obvious – machine tools are different from breakfast cereals – but below that level distinctions can become very blurred. Take, for example, a company with spray-drying technology producing food products sold through the grocery trade. Does such a company concentrate on its technology as arbiter of 'existing markets'? – if so, it could well envisage the development of a spray-dried paint for sale through hardware stores; or is it a food company? – in which case it might be right to look at the possibility of new products in aseptic cans or soy products, or take-away food; or is it a grocery company? – in which case it might be right to concentrate on those markets which are becoming increasingly dominated by grocery distribution such as confectionery, cigarettes and vegetables.

It is obviously necessary to have a systematic approach to the definition of markets of interest.[1] The broad strokes of such a definition will have been set in the course of the company's evaluation process – in the above example the company may well have categorised itself as a food company first, a grocery distribution company second, and a powder products company third. But even with such a specific definition, the number of markets that are 'existing' (in the sense that the company is currently equipped, to at least some degree, to enter them) is legion, and sub-market definitions then come crowding in. One method of evaluating markets can be described as follows:

● Identify the markets or product categories which conceivably could be of interest, but do not attempt to apply too high a level of critical judgement at this stage.

● Specify the basic criteria against which these markets or categories should be assessed, for example:[2]

   — Market size
   — Market growth
   — Market stability
   — User stratification
   — Requirement for special production resources
   — Average gross margins applicable
   — Ease of entry, that is, degree and nature of competition
   — Service levels required
   — Rate of product innovation

[1]See also *Planning a Diversification Strategy*, Occasional Paper published by Industrial Market Research Ltd., London.
[2]For a full list see Aubrey Wilson, *The Art and Practice of Marketing*, Hutchinson (London, 1971), chapter 7.

— Distribution patterns and appropriateness of existing sales organisations to these channels
— Level and nature of promotional activity.

● Assign a points rating to each of the basic criteria, for example:
Size of market:

| | |
|---|---|
| over £10 million at selling price | 40 |
| £5–£10 million at selling price | 20 |
| £1–£5 million at selling price | 10 |
| under £1 million at selling price | 0 |

Market growth:

| | |
|---|---|
| over 5 per cent per year | 10 |
| 2–5 per cent per year | 5 |
| under 2 per cent per year | 0 |

● Evaluate in terms of the degree of re-orientation necessary for the company to enter the market or category. Again, assign a points rating, such as:

| | |
|---|---|
| nil, or minimum re-orientation required | 0 |
| moderate re-orientation required | −15 |
| major re-orientation required | −30 |

A calculation of the points scored by each of the markets or categories examined will give a ranking which can then be assessed in the light of any other factors which are not so easily quantified, such as trading agreements, government restrictions and intelligence concerning other companies' interest in the area.

The adoption of some kind of systematic technique for market evaluation allows for a more objective and wide-ranging assessment of opportunity areas (although the allocation of points must be qualitative) and looks at all areas with the same yardsticks and comparison baselines. Furthermore, it is not an expensive exercise; some senior management time is, of course, required to set up the criteria, but much of the work of compilation can be done by a more junior employee drawing on published sources such as Government food survey reports, the Census of Production and Business Monitor Reports and published market analyses.[1] More detailed information on a short list of promising areas in the grocery business can be purchased from companies carrying out retail audits, at reasonable cost. And, of course, an advertising agency or market research company would be prepared, for a fee, to compile market analyses drawing on their greater knowledge of published material available.[2]

[1]For example those published by Mintel and the U.S. Bureau of Commerce.
[2]A full checklist of sources of market data is given in chapter 5 ('Marketing Research on a Small Budget'), p. 93.

## Stages of New Product Development

Having identified the main areas in which the company could and would be happy to operate, the scene is set for starting on the development process. There are normally seven development stages: idea generation, concept evaluation, early development, advanced development, market planning, test marketing and national launch.

Although practices differ widely between the development of industrial and consumer products, all new product development projects will pass progressively through some or each of these stages, with the possible exception of test marketing. Test marketing is covered in detail in chapter 4, and it is sufficient here to say only that the company's assessment of risk and/or competitive intentions may lead it to judge that this stage should be omitted.

In reality, distinctions between the different stages become blurred and the main value of viewing the process in a structural way is that it provides both a budgeting and control mechanism. By recognising the character of each stage, in terms of workload and likely costs involved, it becomes easier to schedule a complete programme and to establish review dates and cut-off points. This is of particular value to the smaller company which must continuously ensure that the programme is not getting out of hand.

Before going on to discuss each of the stages up to test marketing in more detail, it is worthwhile looking briefly at the two development methods most commonly used.

## Methods of New Product Development

The two basic ways of organising for new product development can be termed the 'shotgun technique' and the 'rifle technique'.

*The shotgun technique* – This starts from the basic theory that product development is a funnelling operation: that at each development stage the ideas list will become smaller as further work progressively eliminates the non-starters, for production, competitive or financial reasons. Recognising the in-market failure rate of new products, it propounds that, for every successful product, if the development man has four at test market stage, he will need something like eight at market planning, sixteen at advanced development, thirty-two at early development and sixty-four at concept stage. This obviously involves a large and unwieldy programme which is expensive to run. It does, however, provide a programme with, hopefully, some built-in insurance against failure at the varying stages, and a stop/go development programme.

*The rifle technique* – This concentrates from the outset on a very limited list of new products that promise above average chances of success. Whereas the shotgun technique does not attempt to apply very rigorous tests to product ideas at the early stages, because of the risk that ideas may be rejected for the wrong reasons, the rifle technique takes this risk on the basis that market knowledge will permit limited early assessment to override statistical averages. The major risk is, of course, that subsequent proof that this judgement was mistaken can leave a big hole in the programme whilst it swings back into first gear again.

On balance, the shotgun technique is probably the easiest to administer and more suited to development work outside the scope of the company's present experience, but it is costly. The rifle technique demands much more 'feel' and correct critical judgement to achieve the same result, but the cost of getting there will be very much less. For the manager operating on a small budget, there is no dispute as to the technique he should use, but he must be aware of the extra burden upon him and the fact that he has little room for error.

**Idea Generation**

All forms of marketing activity are a blend of art and science. As marketing increasingly borrows and adapts scientific control procedures and systems from other disciplines – such as decision-making theory, critical path analysis, and computer programming – it would seem that the greatest rewards will go to those companies with the biggest array of scientific approaches, and that because of the costs and scale involved these will be the giant corporations. In some ways this will be true, but only because the corporations are using the best methods open to them to reduce risk. There is nothing to stop the smaller company from culling the most appropriate of these systems for adaptation to their own use at little or no cost. But thankfully, the material with which marketing companies are ultimately dealing, the customers, are far from rational beings who are capable of precise predictability even in the industrial marketing environment. The art in marketing will continue to dominate over science for as long as anyone can foresee, and nowhere is this art at such a premium as in new product development, and within new product development nowhere more than in the creation of product ideas that will eventually turn into tangible goods or services making a profit.

*The Creative Process*

Much has been written that attempts to define and thus harness the creative process, from Arthur Koestler's *The Act of Creation*[1] to the new business presentations of most advertising agencies. The truth is that

[1]Arthur Koestler, *The Act of Creation,* Pan Books (London, 1970).

nobody really knows where an idea originates or how it is conceived, and the nearest we have been able to get is to identify some of the factors that militate against successful idea generation, for example, fear of ridicule, blinkered thought processes and insufficient person-to-person dialogue.

Generally there are two ways in which a scientist investigates physical reality. The first and probably more widely held attitude, certainly among non-scientists, is that within a chosen field he sets about collecting observable, measurable facts, and from the accumulation of facts there somehow emerges a pattern which enables him to postulate a theory. The second is that he begins with intimations of a pattern, has a vision of the theory, and then tests its validity against observable, measurable facts.

Like most double viewpoints, there is truth in each of them. The second view – create an hypothesis and check it – is the one more widely held nowadays amongst scientists themselves. Interestingly, these ways in which a scientist looks at physical reality are substantially the same as those with which a new products man can approach the generation of ideas. These can be termed the 'logical insight' and the 'blinding flash'.

*The Logical Insight*

This method develops hypotheses by the logical arrangement of data. The 'building blocks' are usually pieces of general research, such as attitude and usage studies, menu research and product specifications, which are inspected and cross-analysed for gaps in the market. The cigarette manufacturers use this technique almost exclusively, and the highly successful Player's brands have all been moulded by the painstaking fitting together of pieces of market research information on smokers' habits, fears, economic and social requirements.

Some very sophisticated market research techniques have been developed to help identify market gaps and indicate segmentation opportunities, like factor analysis, but they can only be guidelines – the hypothesis still has to be inferred and a creative jump made, albeit from a carefully researched base.

Idea generation through logical insight requires the prior collection of a great deal of usually very expensive data which the smaller company will not have access to. For this reason alone the manager operating on a restricted budget will almost certainly opt for the second method of idea generation described below.

It is not always necessary, however, to make logical insights from research data. Often, the (deceptively) simple technique of applying undiluted thought power to accumulated experience, in order to 'feel' and estimate the future requirements of one's customer, will begin to point inexorably to a certain development route.

## The Blinding Flash

Despite the apparently derogatory description, most people will recognise the meaning and be able to relate to it. The concept of 'wouldn't it be a good idea if . . .' is a familiar one. In its simplest form, this is the starting point for the great majority of new products and the process is beginning to be formalised to produce a greater range and depth of answer to such an easily posed but notoriously difficult question. Two procedures deserve mention, brainstorming and synectics.

### Brainstorming

The brainstorming technique gathers together, often from within the company, a selection of people from various disciplines, aware of the general background to the issue.[1] They are encouraged to talk round the issue, cross-fertilising it from their different backgrounds, in a 'suspended' atmosphere, that is, with no fear of ridicule or concern about relative status in the hierarchy. These can be extremely useful sessions, with the most unexpected people displaying depths, but the sessions need to be guided by a leader with some experience of handling and directing people in such an unaccustomed atmosphere and who can salvage the pearls from the inevitable dross. Brainstorming is an inexpensive way of generating both initial ideas and triggering valuable trains of thought, particularly if the sessions take place in a congenial atmosphere outside normal working hours.

### Synectics

Synectics[2] is an extension of brainstorming and a relatively new technique encouraging the expression of the creative talents within each of us through lateral thinking.[3] Basically, the theory states that the social and business conformity which we all grow into prevents us from thinking other than logically, and usually down familiar and well-recognised paths. The synectics leader guides his group (which can be of the same kind as for brainstorming) along thought paths which run laterally to the problem in hand and whose relationship to the topic only he knows. This 'creativity by stealth' can produce startling results, but can only be run efficiently by companies specialising in the technique. The services of such organisations tend to be very expensive.

   The hypotheses from the blinding flash source of new product ideas are usually unproven, although substantiation may well be found from existing market research data (but it is always necessary to avoid the pitfalls of post-rationalisation). More usually, these hypotheses need to be tested on a specific basis, by specially designed research.

[1]Theodore Levitt, *Innovation in Marketing*, Pan Books (London, 1968), chapter 6.
[2]W. J. Gordon, *Synectics*, Harper & Row (New York, 1961).
[3]Edward de Bono, *Lateral Thinking*, Ward Lock Educational (London, 1970).

Recognising that the great bulk of new product development work is adaptive, one other source of idea generation should be mentioned.

## Market Scanning

This involves being aware of all new product introductions on as wide a plane as possible, and assessing the most likely candidates in terms of the possible application of their product idea to your own operation. There are now a number of companies specialising in new product digests from both Europe and the United States, which can be used in conjunction with trade journals. Press cutting services will also provide most published material on defined areas of interest.

Market scanning is often pure plagiarism of ideas or hypotheses, but is none the worse for that. For the smaller company, it probably represents the starting point in pulling ideas together, and beginning to structure thoughts on the possible direction of development activity. But beyond this, it can provide a means of learning by the mistakes of others and of pointing to opportunity areas where the initial educational work on the consumer has been done and where a profitable 'No. 2' position might exist.

## Concept Evaluation

Concept evaluation involves the classification, screening and exploration of new product ideas that commonsense, experience and 'feel' have allowed to emanate from the idea generation stage. It is here that the concept is tested, if possible using prototype samples. Concept testing uses market research techniques and is probably the most difficult and problematical area that market research is called on to deal with.[1] Techniques vary widely, from exposure of target consumers to a simple printed description of the product or service to be offered (detailing its key benefits, specifications, method of usage and possibly price) to a video-tape recording treatment showing the product in use, sometimes (in the case of consumer foods) with a brand name and mock-up packaging to aid communication and more carefully illustrate the idea. Costs, of course, vary widely, according to which method is deemed appropriate to the specific idea to be tested and this must be carefully considered before any research is purchased. The most important consideration at this stage (as in all other stages) is to design a test which can be carried out within the budget available, answers the particular questions you have, and does not reject or land the idea for the wrong reasons.

Beyond the difficult task of determining that the concept is correctly evaluated, it is at this stage that initial costings must be undertaken to ensure that further development is justified. As far as the development budget is concerned, incursions on a more or less appreciable scale begin to be made now.

[1]See chapter 5 ('Marketing Research on a Small Budget').

**Early Development**

Having determined that the idea is at least broadly in line with a market
need, and that it is viable on a 'first look' financial assessment, customer
acceptance is now checked via small-scale use testing. This enables any
problems of the product in use to be identified and gives broad guidance
on particular product attributes – specification, size, price, packaging,
etc. – so that more refined technical objectives can be set. More precise
product costings can now be made, together with the definition of broad
capital requirements. All of the experience gained on the product can now
be pooled – from the marketing, technical, financial and operational
areas – to help guide the decision as to whether or not the product should
go forward to be included in the product range, in the knowledge that
this requires increasing development expenditure.[1]

**Advanced Development**

At this stage, customer testing on a broad scale by field trials with validated
product prototypes is required.[2] The product is now being honed down
and fine-tuned in its critical areas. This usually requires larger sample
sizes than those used in the blunter assessments required for the early
development stage, though industrial field trials are usually carried out
on a substantially smaller scale than the testing of consumer products. It
is at this stage that pilot production may be required, for example, for a
new chemical product. Again, it is important to examine critically the type
and scale of information required (action standards should be set to
evaluate the results) and not to indulge in the costly pastime of collecting
tangential, 'warm-feeling' data.

A full business analysis can be started, together with the close definition
of production processing, and even packaging requirements can be
commenced at the same time as customer testing. Other departments
in the company are now being involved on a heavy workload basis, and
the 'hidden' costs of new product development will begin to climb. These
must be known and accounted for.

It is usually during the advanced development stage that the advertising
agency will become closely involved (although some companies make a
practice of involving their agency much earlier, particularly since some
rely heavily on their agency for both idea generation and concept evaluation). The not insignificant costs of an agency must now be reckoned
with – however most agencies will work on a negotiated fee basis which
should represent a break-even position for them. They will absorb the

[1] A format for collecting and analysing this information is given by Margot Newlands,
'Organisation of New Product Development', *The Marketing of Industrial Products*,
ed. Aubrey Wilson, Pan Books (London, 1972), pp. 70–9.
[2] See chapter 4 ('Test Marketing in the Low Budget Marketing Mix').

opportunity cost of using costly personnel, against the possibility of future returns from enhanced fees or commission.

At the conclusion of the advanced development stage, the product (or brand, as it by that time should have become) should be completely identified and ready, with only the fine brush strokes remaining to be completed.

## Market Planning

The business analysis outlined during the product's advanced development stage should now be finalised, leading to a full-scale long-term plan (the time scale to be dependent on the company's normal practice, but no less than three years would probably be appropriate) involving volume and financial estimates. The operations feasibility study should be completed at this stage, capital requirements finalised and orders placed for long lead-time machinery.[1] (In many instances, the lead-time involved in securing machinery is such that an order needs to be placed well before this juncture, underlining once again the necessity for as much accuracy as the situation will allow at all development stages.) The timetable to national launch should also now be prepared.

Chapter 4 deals with test marketing and the reader should refer there for information on this complex and potentially costly exercise. However, in terms of the development stages up to test marketing and national launch, control is vital not only to the number and complexity of projects on hand, but also to the many facets of any particular project. This is particularly important when working on a small budget. The best method of control is via a network or critical path analysis. The construction of, and adherence to, a precise critical path analysis will show dividends in three key areas: (i) it allows those responsible for the development of new products to control the various inputs to the plan; (ii) it avoids duplication of activity, thereby optimising use of scarce resources and avoiding the use of unnecessary expensive activities; (iii) it enables risk areas to be highlighted so that appropriate option planning can be made. The time span for a product to come through the idea generation stage to the completion of market planning will vary from one year in the case of food products, to up to ten years in the case of complex industrial products. In some circumstances, the development period can be substantially reduced if a higher level of risk is accepted which could be acceptable in specific competitive situations, and in others, where for example a new technology is involved, it can be very appreciably longer. The development of Kesp, the spun-fibre meat substitute by Courtaulds, would certainly be in the latter category. But Bird's Mellow coffee, because of a specific competitive situation that required fast action to capitalise on an oppor-

[1]Margot Newlands, *op. cit.*

tunity, was initiated, developed and distributed nationally in under twelve months.

## Financial Criteria

For those operating a new products programme on a small budget it is crucial to have made two related sets of decisions: the total amount of money to be invested, and the criteria for evaluating new products.

### Total Amount to be Invested

Development costs should not be offset against projected future returns as these may never occur. Development money in this context (people costs, market research costs, agency costs, etc.) must be treated as an affordable loss – it is gambling money and the prime maxim in that related business is, as far as the punter is concerned, never to pay out more than you can afford to lose. The expenditure should, of course, be planned to take account of the different phases of the development process. A project will not, for example, incur advertising development costs if it fails at the concept evaluation or in-home use testing stages. A schedule can be drawn up which will reasonably accurately indicate costs under different assumptions (of success/failure at varying stages) and this should be the basis for arriving at the development budget.[1]

It is a hard decision to accept that this budget could represent a loss in its entirety, and no product development man when asking for funds can find it easy to make the point. He will, understandably, talk in terms of the returns to be expected from this investment and he is employed, amongst other things, to be forward-looking and optimistic. But it is vital that the company isolates today's investment, which will directly affect the profit and loss account, from the seductive beckonings of jam tomorrow.

### Criteria for Evaluating New Products

It is surprising to note the number of otherwise sophisticated companies who approach the evaluation of each new project on an *ad hoc* basis. The establishment of at least broad financial guidelines for new products gives the product development man a set of objectives which he can himself apply at all stages, and saves the company's management from having to make what are often rushed, emotional or otherwise ill-conceived assessments when the time for a go/no-go decision is reached. It is impossible, of course, to be specific, but some general guidelines can be laid down to aid the establishment of financial criteria.

### A New Product should not dilute present Company Performance

This is particularly true in the key areas of the gross margin and return

[1]Margot Newlands, *op. cit.*

on funds employed, but tests should also be applied to other areas such as company headcount, cashflow, inventory, receivables, etc.

### Target Performances must be set

Arising from the general requirement not to dilute present company performance, a specific return on funds employed and payback target should be set from which departures can be assessed and judged. For example, it could be that a project does not meet these targets, but its value to the business is great in other respects – such as a contribution to already existing fixed costs, trade/consumer image and competitive pre-emption. It makes life much easier, and the judgement more meaningful, if comparison can be made with a base-line, and the extent of the gap 'quantified'.

### Minimise Risk

The techniques that give marketing the aura of scientific exactitude are all designed to aid in the vital task of minimising risk. In new product development a project's returns are often in direct correlation with the risk involved. Those operating on a small budget must be aware of the risk elements in two respects. First, the amount of risk which they as a company are prepared to accept in general (the prime order of risk) and no guideline can be set for that. Second, and more immediate, the techniques available for quantifying and, therefore, being able to hedge against the risks inherent in any individual project (the secondary order of risk). These techniques vary from financial controls – running schedules of commitment and cancellation costs for capital items and revenue items (raw materials, packaging materials, etc.) – to option planning of the type to provide answers to such questions as: what would be the withdrawal costs in the event of total failure? what is the break-even point for sales and how does this compare with the volume targets for the project? what are the implications of, say, a 25 per cent increase in raw material costs? Sensitivity analysis, the technique for determining the relative impact on results of changes in the different variables in the mix, is a powerful tool for identifying key risk areas from which the scale of secondary order risks can be assessed.

The criteria for judging new products should contain a statement of the company's stance with regard to prime order risks, and as far as possible guidelines on the way in which it expects secondary order risks to be controlled.

### Allocation of Overheads to New Projects

Many a promising idea has been suffocated at birth because of an accountant who, on the first tentative financial plan for a new product, has allocated not only its own 'incremental' fixed costs but also its share of total company fixed overheads. This often 'proves' that a new product is not viable and consequently there is a disinclination to do further work on the project. Obviously, one must be aware of the incremental fixed costs that the product will attract, but an attempt should be made to keep this running in parallel until the product opportunity has been fully explored. As far as allocated fixed costs are concerned, it is advisable to work the new product's profit and loss account to contribution level only, and to decide when (or if) the product should carry full fixed cost allocation.

## The Scale of New Products

The scale of new products, in terms of initial development investment, marketing support and turnover required, depends almost entirely on the size and attitude of the company developing them. But in any situation, the temptation must be avoided to set impossibly high volume targets. Any deficiency in a new product plan can be eliminated, or substantially reduced, by increasing the volume target. Setting this target is the key to the plan, and this may be determined according to prevailing conditions: if the product is to enter an established market with entrenched competition, assumptions have to be made regarding the business that will be taken from other brands; if the product is opening a new market, the effect on market growth of the product's own presence, competitive interest, and so on. Every effort should be made to test the volume assumptions, and these efforts do not cost money, just thought and commonsense.

Starting with the customers, check what they are being asked to do; for example, how many housewives or potential industrial users are required to try your product (and over what period) to provide the base from which the 'going' business will be generated? How much are you asking a user to consume in a week, a month, a year? What stocks will the user carry? On the distribution front, what rate of sale by the various types of outlet does the volume target pre-suppose? How does this compare with the trade's own assessment of acceptable turnover in related product fields? What levels of shop and warehouse stock are involved? It is useful to bear in mind that distributors' decisions to stock, and continue to stock, a new product depend both on their assessment of customer appeal (and therefore, rate of sale) and on their own profit margin expectations. They are willing to accept a lower-than-average rate of return on fast moving products such as instant coffee or industrial fastenings, but will demand very much higher returns on more specialised, slow-moving lines such as spices, or electric motors. Trade margin is therefore an important regulator and a useful test to apply to volume assumptions.

It is often considered that a high level of marketing investment is a necessary concomitant to the launch of a new product, particularly in the fast-moving consumer goods area. Certainly, high marketing expenditure should create high awareness and, hopefully, high disposition to buy, both with the consumer and the trade, and there are many markets where the entrance fee has to be reckoned in hundreds of thousands of pounds. However, whilst the availability of a large budget is in some cases mandatory (and reassuring!), in many others it is not. Two important points should be made, which whilst applicable to new product development on any scale, are particularly pertinent to those working on small budgets:

● No amount of marketing expenditure can paper over the cracks of product deficiency. What it can do is accelerate and magnify a business that would otherwise still have existed; the product must be good enough to sell on its own merits.

● The level of marketing investment behind a new product should be *a separate investment decision.* It is important to separate the product opportunity from the marketing support and identify the scale of business that a new product would achieve by virtue of its answer to a consumer need. This might seem a hypothetical and valueless exercise, but its importance lies in the fact that, having done it, you can be assured that a *real* product opportunity exists (as opposed to a marketing-supported artefact) and can then begin to make assessments of the investment needed to gain maximum distribution and accelerate the business.

The data input would be market research, particularly for assessing 'base' volume, and a mixture of market research and perhaps area testing for the level of marketing spend.

The important points to be made are that substantial marketing funds are not a prerequisite for new product success, and that the scale and timing of marketing investment must be approached on the same basis, and with the same searching scrutiny, as that for the project as a whole.

### Avoiding Wastage

New product development is a potentially costly exercise, particularly if there is no return from a finally marketed product to offset development expenditure.

However, as has been indicated throughout this chapter there are ways to limit exposure. These can be grouped under two general headings: knowing what is wanted and controlling what is being done.

### *Knowing What is Wanted*

One of the biggest cash drains in new product development stems from imprecisely defined objectives. On the one hand, too many projects at varying stages often lead to insufficient time being spent on analysing, nurturing and 'feeling' any individual project. On the other, too few projects and the consequent reliance on them to 'come good' often means a costly change of gear when this does not happen. A balanced programme, both in terms of number of projects and spacing throughout the development programme, is the best way of avoiding the dangers of extreme. The precise composition of the optimum programme will obviously depend on the company and the scale of resources it chooses to make available.

Similarly, market research expenditure is a significant portion of the development budget, and can entail a great deal of wastage through imprecise objectives and over elaborate techniques.[1]

*Controlling What is Being Done*

Many control systems can be utilised to minimise risk, identify potential high cost areas, evaluate alternative activities and help formalise decision-making. A number have been touched on in this chapter – such as critical path analysis, value analysis, sensitivity analysis, running commitment and cancellation schedules. Whilst, as in any business, it is more than valuable to keep abreast of new developments, it is not necessary to know in great detail all the control systems available. The knowledge that they exist, and broadly what area of the programme they help in, is often sufficient to be able to tailor a simple system that adequately controls the activity for the company concerned.

**Getting the Job Done**

One of the greatest problems for the smaller company is to know how to go about providing for the different inputs to new product development. The first question is whether to have a new products man on the payroll, or to contract out all the development work either to an advertising agency with new product workshop facilities, or to a company specialising in new product work. When embarking for the first time on a new products programme, it is better to 'sub-contract' until it becomes clear that the volume of work, and indeed the general direction of activities, justifies the employment of a specialist. Additional fixed costs should be avoided until they can be adequately covered; in the meantime, it is probably advisable to contract out as many requirements as possible on a short-term basis, although the costs will be higher. When and if a new products specialist on the payroll is required, his selection is not likely to be easy. Good development personnel are hard to find, first, because the function is still imperfectly understood, even in the most development-orientated companies, and second, because the function is probably the most difficult that anyone is asked to perform. To do a good development job requires complete knowledge of the mechanics of product development; additionally, it needs creative feel and an imperviousness to frustration not required by other managers in the company. Such people are difficult to locate,

[1]A full discussion of the methods of minimising research expenditure will be found in chapter 5 ('Marketing Research on a Small Budget').

and their suitability can only really be judged from an intensive interview situation, with a thorough checklist of job requirements as related to the company as an interview guide.

As regards technical development work, the pros and cons of setting up an R & D department must be weighed very carefully.[1] If there are any doubts about the scope or duration of the R & D job required, the work can be sub-contracted to a laboratory institute or research agency on a specified fee.

Very often the capital costs associated with manufacturing a new product present the biggest problem to the smaller company. There is understandable concern about putting scarce capital resources behind an untried idea, and consequent difficulty in raising sufficient financial backing without jeopardising part of the existing business base. Co-manufacturing or co-packing provides an answer, giving time to read the new product's level of success or failure before capital commitment whilst retaining control of marketing. Unless the process is entirely new, spare manufacturing or packing capacity can usually be located. Of course, the benefit of a manufacturer's margin is lost, but in many cases this is an acceptable short-term offset to high capital risk, and may indeed be the only feasible method in the early stages. However, the difficulties in negotiating and maintaining acceptable prices, quality and delivery dates should be recognised together with the danger of handing a 'property' to a third party who, if you are not well protected, could become a competitor.

Even in the age of the giant corporation, new inventions, processes or other technological breakthroughs often come from the small company. Sometimes these are of a potential scale far beyond the resources of the company concerned. Licensing or know-how agreements can be negotiated, which will usually cover both manufacture and marketing and thus involve little or no capital investment. But there must exist real rights to the business in question, in the form of a patent, registered design, trademark or exclusive know-how and a licensing agreement will have a specific life, usually the life of the patent. Licensing agreements are particularly valuable where an invention needs to be launched quickly, and, perhaps, simultaneously in many countries, but the returns will almost always be less than would be gained from own manufacture. However, in many situations there is little choice and the income from licensing agreements is an extremely useful cash source, as well as a valuable asset against which to raise finance for other parts of the business (particularly if negotiated with well-known, financially stable companies). There are many arrangements possible for payment of manufacturing and marketing rights, but they centre around lump sum or royalty payments, or some combination of both. It is important to select a payment system which best complements the current and future cash needs of your business.

[1] See chapter 3 ('Research and Development on a Small Budget').

The main burden of 'getting the job done' rests with the senior management of the company. In a large or a small enterprise, the organisation responds to and reflects the direction and enthusiasm of its senior management. There is no substitute for the direct, enthusiastic involvement of the chief executive – he must make it clear by both word and action that he intends to see that the very difficult new product development activity happens. Apathy or obvious lack of involvement on his part is certain, in the context of day-to-day pressures from the existing business, to turn the development effort into a sterile exercise.

## CHECKLIST

● Have precise medium and long-term objectives been set for the company?

● Are you getting the most out of your present business?

● What is the extent of the need for new products and have all alternative methods of obtaining growth been evaluated?

● Have new product objectives been set?

● Have the existing and potential markets for the new products been satisfactorily investigated?

● Has customer acceptance of the new products been tested?

● Have realistic and achievable financial targets been set for the new products which will neither dilute current profit performance nor overstretch the resources available (production, marketing and financial)?

● Have suitable control mechanisms been set up to control the budget outlay on new products?

● At what point will further investment in the new products (development and marketing) be cut and against what criteria will this decision be taken?

● Has the risk of failure of the new products been evaluated and contingency plans laid? Are the losses which will be incurred in the event of a failure affordable?

● Have potential sub-contractors for development work been identified and evaluated?

● Have potential licensors, licencees and joint venture partners been identified?

CHAPTER 3

# Research and Development on a Small Budget

By Brian Fletcher

The potential contribution which research and development (R & D) can make to the successful marketing of any product or enterprise frequently is not realised by marketing men and the subject often is paid scant attention except when a crisis threatens. In part, this reflects a failure to appreciate what R & D is all about and a consequent tendency to pay too much attention to the costs and too little to the returns. It may also be an example of C. P. Snow's 'two cultures', a direct consequence of the fact that the majority of marketing men have little if any scientific training.

For this misunderstanding, the profession itself has much to answer for. The high cost of research, particularly on projects which fail, receives much publicity. So, too, do the assertions that as a nation we do not spend enough on R & D. By contrast, too little is heard of the successes which result from sensible application of R & D resources. To gain a more balanced perspective, it might be helpful, therefore, at the outset to deal with some of the most popular misconceptions which colour the thinking of many business enterprises about the value of R & D.

## The Value of Research and Development

Of all business activities, R & D is the most obviously feminine – intensely frustrating, extremely demanding and occasionally rewarding. In more prosaic language, it must often seem to a layman that the costs of R & D far outweigh the benefits. Certainly, he might be forgiven for concluding, on reading of the £1,000 million plus spent on Concorde, that R & D is increasingly becoming the prerogative of the 'big spenders'. For a company operating with a limited R & D budget (the rule rather than the exception), this conclusion, if correct, has disturbing implications. At the outset therefore the argument on which it is based demands critical examination.

In its exploded form, it runs as follows:

● Successful R & D requires an abundance of both inventiveness and financial resources.

● Most (small) companies lack one or both of these prerequisites.

● Since their efforts can in consequence be only partially successful at best, and since their competitors are in any case in a similar position, why bother with the problems involved in attempting to conduct R & D 'on a shoe-string'?

Thus stated, the argument is persuasive, but fallacious.

Successful R & D does not demand high inventiveness. Although many of today's most successful companies owe their fortunes to the invention of a particular product or process – Pilkington and Polaroid are two outstanding examples – the adage that genius is 1 per cent inspiration and 99 per cent perspiration was never more true than of R & D. Of course, it helps to have a da Vinci on one's staff, but inventiveness is not an essential prerequisite for a successful R & D programme.

Furthermore, successful R & D does not necessarily demand abundant financial resources. At first sight published statistics on R & D expenditure can appear daunting. ICI are reported to spend over £60 million a year; Hoechst, employing over 10,000 people in R & D, spend a similar amount, as do Hoffman La Roche, the world's largest pharmaceutical company. In total, over £300 million was spent on pharmaceutical research in the United States alone in 1971. In other fields, the expenditure figures are even more astronomical: IBM are reported to have spent over £2,000 million developing the series 360 computer. The need for investment on this scale in turn creates pressure for concentration within the particular industry, whether through merger (a major justification for the abortive Beecham bid for Glaxo was stated to be the opportunity for improving returns on R & D), the growth of multi-national companies, or State take-over of particular industries judged to be vital to the national interest, e.g. aircraft and computers. Figure 3.1 opposite shows the relationship between R & D expenditures and sales by industrial sector.

Clearly, the market characteristics of particular industries compel massive investment, although for every British Leyland there are a host of smaller satellite companies each of whom require an R & D facility appropriate to the size of the enterprise. By contrast, the R & D turnover ratio for the food and tobacco industries, and indeed for most consumer goods, is and always has been very modest. Given that within any one industry the ratio tends to be reasonably constant for all firms, then by definition there is a direct correlation between the size of the company and the absolute level of R & D expenditure. However, as most readers will be quick to avow, there is no causal relationship between size and success in business. This being so, there is no reason in principle why

FIGURE 3.1.

*R & D Intensity by Industrial Sector*

| R & D AS PERCENT NET OUTPUT | SECTOR |
| --- | --- |
| Over 10% | Aerospace, electronics, telecommunications, mineral oil refining |
| 4 to 10% | Plastics, pharmaceuticals, motor vehicles |
| 2 to 4% | Electrical & mechanical engineering, textile and agricultural machinery, domestic appliances |
| 1 to 2% | Textiles and man-made fibres, food, drink, tobacco |

*Source:* Centre for Study of Industrial Innovation

any company, irrespective of size, should not be able to maintain a leve of R & D support proportionate to the industry ratio.

Furthermore, although large firms can obviously spare greater resources for R & D and can bear larger risks, small firms have two distinct advantages. First, large firms tend to be bureaucratic and hierarchical, both of which have a dampening effect on inventiveness. In addition, hierarchical organisations have long memories for mistakes and the larger the hierarchy the greater the chance that someone will veto a development programme.[1]

### The Need for Research and Development

The argument so far has demonstrated that small companies can afford to maintain an R & D facility. It is further contended that no company, large or small, which wishes to stay in business can afford not to have an R & D facility. Arguably, this was less true a hundred or even fifty years ago, but today when, as the Red Queen said, 'here . . . it takes all the running you can do to keep in the same place', the businessman who fails to make use of R & D is operating at a severe disadvantage. Paradoxically, the two key reasons why, more than ever, R & D is necessary appear at first sight to be in opposition.

First, business is increasingly fettered. From the *laissez-faire* attitude of the early nineteenth century there has been steadily increasing intervention both from government and other pressure groups to protect the consumer, whether individually or en masse, against the more harmful side-effects of industrialisation. This trend has intensified over the past decade and there are a number of factors which strongly suggest that the constraints will increase rather than diminish. In every industry, therefore, the businessman must not only ensure that the products he manufactures today conform with the myriad regulations and controlling standards but, perhaps even more important, he must anticipate the social implications of technical change. They might provide him with a new business opportunity or conversely, if he fails to recognise them, force him out of business. In this situation, R & D acts as an early warning system and as such can be regarded as an insurance against extinction.

Second, business is increasingly competitive. The 'seat of the pants' approach to business with entrepreneurs acting on instinct with Olympian disregard of the small-minded antics of their competitors, has always had a beguiling appeal. However, as a formula for success its reliability must always have been questionable: in today's environment it is an infallible recipe for disaster. In particular, the failure to use R & D when one's competitors are doing so is a crippling handicap, the worse for being self-imposed.

Increasingly, firms large and small are *consciously* setting objectives

[1]David Fishlock, 'Examining Research in Business', *The Financial Times*, 11 September, 1974.

and devising strategies to meet them. To a businessman who seeks a profitable growth at the expense of his competitors, R & D is an essential tool. Elmshurst, the founder and inspiration of the highly imaginative and successful Dartington project,[1] has stressed the vital role played by research in enabling him to transform a bankrupt and demoralised farming community in Devon in the late nineteen-twenties into a thriving business enterprise whose products have earned world-wide renown.

To the converted, all this may seem an unnecessarily prolonged state-ment of the obvious. However, a recent report[2] by the Chairman of the National Research Development Corporation is typical of the concern being voiced from every quarter. He refers to 'a reluctance on the part of industry to become involved in the financing of long-term projects, or to raise the level of its support of its own research and development pro-grammes to keep pace with cost inflation'.

As might be expected it is the small and medium-sized companies who have tended to neglect R & D. There are of course honourable excep-tions, for example Lintolt Engineering, an old-established iron-founding concern in Sussex who sponsored a joint venture with Harwell which paid off in the successful development of a highly sophisticated machine tool. Most small firms, however, find a variety of reasons for not engaging in R & D. Predominant amongst them is the concern that research costs too much. This concern betrays an attitude of mind which regards R & D as inherently uncontrollable and therefore not subject to normal business disciplines. Contrast this with the assertion by ICI's Research Director, that 'research has a purpose, to produce a profit', a philosophy which all companies could with advantage adopt.

## Maximising Returns from Research and Development

Stripped to its essentials, the task of maximising the returns from R & D is critically dependent on three factors: (i) matching objectives with resources; (ii) establishment of an effective control system; and (iii) assiduous exploitation of R & D output.

### Matching Objectives to Meet Resources

One of the most frequently recurring questions with which any R & D manager is confronted is 'Are we spending too much/enough/too little on research?' Despite the frequency with which the question is asked, the answer is rarely satisfactory. Too often there is a discussion of the need to ensure that R & D expenditure as a percentage of turnover maintains a constant relationship to previous years or to the average for the industry.

[1]A successful complex of educational, rural-industrial and cultural activities, introduced in order to revitalise rural life in the area of Dartington.
[2]National Research Development Corporation, *Annual Report 1971 to 1972*, HMSO (London, 1973).

Important though such comparisons are in the long term, such an approach to the determination of the resources needed provides only very broad parameters and, more important, it fails to realise that the original question is incomplete. To permit a more meaningful dialogue, the question should read something like '*Are we spending too much/enough/too little on research to give ourselves a reasonable chance of achieving our objectives?*'

Addressed in these terms, the R & D manager can begin to assess whether the available resources – people, equipment and funds – are sufficient to carry out the agreed work programme. Before doing so, however, he must satisfy himself that the objectives set for his own department are consistent with the overall objectives of the company. In this respect the small company with shorter lines of communication is, or should be, at an advantage. The role of planning in helping to suggest viable alternative directions for a business has been discussed in chapter 2. At this juncture it is sufficient to observe that since the extent to which a particular company chooses to be an innovator rather than to be an exploiter of other people's ideas will affect both the absolute amount spent on R & D and the nature and emphasis of the work itself, the definition and communication of the company's objectives are responsibilities which can and must be discharged by the senior management group within the company before individual departmental objectives can be established.

The definition of specific research objectives flowing from the overall business strategy may be by type of activity, e.g. product improvement, cost reduction, new product development, or in terms of particular projects, e.g. to reduce the raw material costs of Brand $X$ by 5 per cent without impairing product quality. Whichever approach is adopted it is essential to ensure that the objectives are not established *in vacuo* but are related as closely as possible to identified consumer needs. Many of the extravagant benefits promised from the broad-scale adoption of a 'marketing orientated' approach by United Kingdom industry have proved illusory, but one thing which marketing men can fairly claim is to have disciplined businessmen to look at their product through the eyes of the eventual user.

The penalties of neglecting this discipline seem obvious, yet case histories abound of the lesson having been forgotten or never learned, even among large organisations. Consider, for example, the classic case of the National Coal Board, an organisation spending more than £2·5 million a year on research for the 250 collieries still open, which developed at its research centre a coal-cutting machine tailored to the requirements of one pit and unsuited to any other coal face in Britain. Admittedly there are occasions, particularly in the area of new product development, where the businessman is gambling on consumers discovering a need for his product which did not exist previously. In practice, however, intelligent use of market research should enable one to discover, at an early stage, whether or not there is a 'latent' demand – indeed the absence of any such indication can be taken as a danger signal that the particular idea may have a very minority appeal.

R & D then, in terms of both scale and direction, should be consistent with the overall business objectives and strategy. With these broad parameters identified it should then be possible to establish specific R & D objectives, either by activity type or by project, which reflect known consumer needs. At this stage and not before, it is possible to judge whether the objectives match the resources and vice versa. If they do, well and good. If not, then by definition additional resources must be found or a less ambitious R & D programme be adopted.

*Establish an Effective Control System*

Having identified, whether by good fortune or painful compromise, a set of objectives which appear realistic in relation to available resources, the next step is to set up a satisfactory day-to-day control system.

**The Control of R & D**

To suggest the need for such a system invites the response, particularly in the case of companies whose research department is a one-man show, that this implies further additions to fixed overheads, and as such increases rather than reduces the cost of R & D. It is true that some of the larger companies are able and feel compelled by their size to make use of computer-based planning tools, such as linear programming, as aids in the monitoring of their research activity. Clearly, the smaller and simpler the research programme, the less need there is for a formalised control system. However, the disciplines involved can with advantage be applied irrespective of size. At its simplest the system should provide a framework to help determine *what to do*, and *how to do it*. In many instances, this may imply no more than an annual exercise by the research manager to spell out, to the satisfaction of himself and his colleagues, that there is a sensible balance between work to be done, time allowed and resources required. Thus stated, the suggestion appears obvious; from observation, however, the absence of a satisfactory control system, often justified on the basis that 'scientists can't produce their best work in such circumstances', makes it impossible to distinguish between necessary and unnecessary expenditure, and as such is a prime cause of waste of resources.

**Research Objectives and Means**

The need for a clear definition of R & D objectives has been argued at length. In defining them, the manager responsible must be on guard against the danger of assuming too readily that all the work involved in fulfilling these objectives must be undertaken by the company's own R & D department – indeed there are usually good reasons why this should not be so. As a generalisation, there is considerable duplication of R & D effort across industry, particularly amongst big companies who at the same time complain of the high fixed cost of research. The justification most commonly advanced to explain this paradox is the need to preserve security to protect one's competitive position. Without denying the validity of this argument, it is nonetheless difficult to resist the conclusion that a high price is being paid for an often illusory peace of mind. The proposed Beecham/Glaxo merger referred to earlier, represented one attempt to resolve this dilemma: presumably the decision taken by Volkswagen and Daimler in the mid nineteen-sixties to collaborate on basic research was, at least partly, motivated by recognition of this problem.

By contrast, the small businessman, with perhaps little or no fixed R & D costs, has a degree of flexibility which he would be wise to preserve. He should recognise that over-investment in R & D means high on-going costs or, more likely, the need for a severe cut-back once the 'initial' programme has been completed – the 'stop go' syndrome which is notoriously wasteful of resources. Instead, he should consider carefully;

● What work has to be done?

● By whom?

● How much of it has he/must he get the resources to undertake?

● Conversely, what portion is he prepared to farm out, e.g. to government, industry or university research departments?

Paradoxically, companies with limited R & D facilities, who potentially have most to gain from 'contract research', make comparatively little use of it. The various reasons advanced – security risk, cost, laced frequently with personal pride – are understandable, but the sensible businessman, concerned to get full value for every pound spent on R & D, would be well-advised to find out what help can be obtained from outside, particularly where the security risk is slight, or when the work is of a one-off nature for which it is not worthwhile equipping. Used sensibly, contract research permits companies with limited R & D resources to keep up with the 'knowledge explosion' which Alvin Tofler[1] and others have so vividly depicted and thereby to counter the potential advantage which the industrial giants might gain through size alone.[2]

---

[1]Alvin Tofler, *Future Shock,* Pan Books (London, 1971).
[2]Interested readers are referred to a useful catalogue of outside facilities to be found in a handbook published by the Department of Trade and Industry in 1970 entitled *Technical Services for Industry,* which lists all the various research services available from government departments together with all the industrial research associations.

## The Management of R & D

It can be assumed that, by this point, the company management has decided what its R & D objectives are and by careful planning or extreme good fortune has provided itself with appropriate resources in terms of people (including the use of outside facilities) and equipment and funds. Why not leave the department to get on with it? – after all, scientists are paid to be creative. The danger of such a *laissez-faire* approach can perhaps best be illustrated from the analyses undertaken by Booz, Allen and Hamilton[1] in the area of new product development. It has become part of marketing folklore that some four out of five new grocery products launched in any one year in the US or UK (and the pattern is probably true of most other markets) will 'fail' – the exact figure will vary depending on definition, time, period, etc., but the general principle is beyond dispute. What is less well known is that 'although the percentage of commercial successes display relatively little variation in terms of sectors they do differ considerably among firms within a given sector. The reason for this can be found in the discernible differences in management from one firm to the next as regards new products'.

The varying success rate for new products is the most conspicuous and telling illustration of the extent to which management efficiencies in all areas, but particularly R & D pays off. It is a truism that greater experience in manufacturing and production ought to be reflected in lower production costs, to the ultimate benefit of one's competitive position. But the operative word is 'ought'; cost reductions have to be made to happen. Thus one of the principal prerequisites for minimising the R & D budget is a strong and effective management system.

The optimum organisation structure and control system for R & D is a difficult area across which to generalise, since much depends on the size of the company. The common aim, however, irrespective of size, must be to 'discipline creativity'. This apparent contradiction in terms has many parallels with the so-called venture management concept currently fashionable in marketing which attempts to introduce into the often rigid, hierarchical organisational structure sufficient flexibility to permit the profitable expression of entrepreneurial skills. Similarly, an unstructured approach to R & D may well lead to a profligate waste of resources for the occasional moment of serendipity. This is not to under-estimate the necessity of idea generation in any R & D programme, nor of the techniques from brainstorming, through synectics to the permanent R & D 'think tank' which the toy manufacturers Denys Fisher were reputed to have established some years ago to capitalise on their success with 'Spirograph' and other educational toys. But for most companies, lack of ideas is not the

[1]Booz, Allen and Hamilton, 'Getting into Shape to Manage New Products', *European Business No. 30* (Summer 1971).

problem: rather, the need is for some system which sorts the wheat from the chaff as early as possible. To this end, management effort should be directed to bring into focus three main issues: (i) ensuring clear definition of responsibilities; (ii) budgetary control; and (iii) staff motivation.

### Definition of Responsibilities

A recurring problem in large companies (and arguably even more so in the companies officially classified as 'small; i.e. with less than 500 employees, which account for over 40 per cent of total industrial production), is to ensure that there is clear understanding where an individual manager's responsibilities begin and end. This problem is particularly acute in areas such as R & D which overlap with marketing on the one hand and production on the other. To what extent, for example, is the R & D department permitted, or indeed expected, to monitor product quality or to initiate work on new product development or cost reduction? Or are these respectively production and marketing department responsibilities? As always, there are no hard and fast rules appropriate for every company.

This is particularly true in smaller organisations where the R & D manager may well double up in some other capacity, e.g. as plant manager. This being so, it is important that a conscious decision should be taken on where the R & D manager's responsibilities begin and end, and that this demarcation line should be reviewed at regular intervals to ensure that it remains in keeping with any changes of objectives or personalities.

As a corollary, having determined the respective spheres of influence of R & D, production and marketing, care must be taken to ensure that there is adequate liaison between these three areas, and indeed between R & D and all other company departments. More will be said later about the typical R & D worker and the extent to which he appears to seek isolation. At this stage it is sufficient to observe, as a generalisation, that imperfect communication of objectives by the 'client' and of results by the R & D department is the root cause of much of the waste of R & D resources which undoubtedly exists.

### Budgetary Control

The R & D manager, in establishing his programme for the next year, must balance three variables: required output, time and cost. The more complex the programme, the greater the need to attempt to prepare a detailed breakdown of estimated time to completion, materials, and labour and hence, ultimately, financial resources required, and to review the progress made on a regular, say, monthly basis. This control process has several benefits:

*It disciplines the department to concentrate resources on specific objectives.* Admittedly, this is more relevant to a programme which is orientated towards applied research although, paradoxically, the old adage 'half funds are wasted but I don't know which half' is probably more true of basic than of applied research.

*It acts as an early warning system to management of departures from plans.* This speaks for itself; regular reviews by project of progress made against objectives and resources used are an obvious means of monitoring the total programme.

*It permits planned re-deployment of funds.* In all likelihood, programme objectives will be modified during the course of the year, new priorities discovered, others, previously identified, changed or discarded. In part, this will be a response to external factors such as government legislation and competitive activity. In part, it will reflect the success or failure of individual elements in the programme. Whatever the reason, the changing objectives will automatically call for a re-appraisal of resources to determine whether in total they are more or less than adequate to meet the new situation, and to examine whether any re-allocation between individual projects is called for.

Some of the larger companies use linear programming, and otners computer-based tools to monitor their R & D activity but firms with small budgets may object that the control process described, however admirable, is far too detailed and, more important, too expensive to meet the needs of their own organisation. The reaction is a healthy one – a multiplication of pro-forma is often a sign of a hardening of the mental arteries frequently accompanied by escalating overheads. But in practice for most organisations, all that is necessary is for the R & D manager to produce and up-date one piece of paper, using a general layout such as that shown in Figure 3.2., tailored to meet individual needs. Even with such a simple planning aid, the manager can determine the adequacy of total resources against objectives, he can develop a project work schedule which relates required man-hours to required completion date and, most important, he has an early warning system to help him identify the critical projects which are taking longer/costing more than originally planned and which in consequence threaten to wreck the programme unless corrective action is taken.

### Staff Motivation

Philip Kotler[1] states that:

the company's most important challenge is to manage R & D effectively. Some managers complain that scientists are not people. Management

[1]Philip Kotler, *Marketing Management: Analysis Planning and Control,* Prentice Hall (Englewood Cliffs, New Jersey, 1972).

and supervision techniques that work in other areas may fail miserably when applied to scientists. Scientists like to set their own objectives, work at their own pace, be surrounded by expensive equipment, and have loose supervision. Yet the downfall of many R & D operations is precisely the lack of supervision, financial control and measurement of results.

Besides reinforcing what has been said about the importance of adequate control, Kotler touches on one of the most critical elements in any R & D programme, most of which are manpower intensive, namely the scientists themselves.

It is a commonplace in any large company to hear it said that the R & D department feels isolated, whether or not any physical separation from the rest of the organisation exists. At root this springs from an insistence by the staff to be taken on their own terms, i.e. the nature of their work tends to encourage innate individualism. Significantly, much of the pilot work on 'flexible timing', i.e. allowing employees some measure of choice of working hours on any particular day, has been carried out in R & D facilities. Indeed, it may well be that the spectacular successes achieved reflect the nature of the group of employees and as such are not reproducible elsewhere in a business organisation.

Paradoxically, despite this tendency towards a self-imposed isolation, researchers at the same time feel the need for security, the reassurance that they belong. The task of channelling the skills of what is generally one of the most highly qualified groups within the company towards the achievement of objectives, with which they are not always in sympathy, whilst at the same time sustaining their creativity, is a very demanding one. This approach will vary according to individual company circumstance: one common element however, irrespective of the size or type of company, is the importance of having a good R & D manager.

It is a calumny that R & D people have neither the inclination nor the aptitude for management. It is undoubtedly true, however, that the man who can motivate an R & D department to achieve results working within the constraints of detailed project briefs and tight budgetary control is a rare individual. He may not necessarily be the best scientist on the payroll, but this is unimportant provided he can command the respect of his staff and harness their specialist abilities to the general good of the company. Depending on the size of the organisation there are a number of techniques the R & D manager can adopt to achieve this goal:

1. He can organise his department on a project rather than function basis – i.e. instead of banding together all the engineers in one group, all the chemists in another, he can create teams with complementary skills to work on particular projects. This not only ensures concentration of R & D resources on those objectives which really matter

| Project | Resources required | | Estimated cost | | Target completion date | Current status vs. Plan |
|---------|--------------------|----|----------------|----|------------------------|-------------------------|
| | Man hours | Materials | Manpower | Materials | | |
| | | | | | | |
| | | | | | | |
| | | | | | | |
| | | | | | | |
| | | | | | | |
| | | | | | | |
| | | | | | | |
| | | | | | | |
| | | | | | | |
| | | | | | | |

FIGURE 3.2.

*Sample R & D Progress Report Format*

and thereby avoids a persistent tendency to re-invent the wheel, it also provides a nucleus for the eventual involvement of managers from other departments and thus helps to facilitate the progress from bench to top commercial application.

2. He can and should ask for a regular, say quarterly, meeting of the senior management group within the company with the specific objective of reviewing progress made, discussing particular problems and opportunities, and ultimately confirming or varying objectives.

3. Perhaps using this management meeting as the vehicle, the R & D manager can consciously seek to ensure that the overall programme reflects a balance between the demands of other departments for R & D services and the supply of new products/ideas arising from the initiative of the R & D department itself.

In all this, the research manager is acting as a bridgehead between his department and the rest of the company. To quote Dr. Rathenau, research chief of Philips, 'research lives on surprise'. The most important thing for a research manager to do is to make sure the surprises are not wasted.

**The Exploitation of Research and Development**

The first two stages in ensuring a successful R & D programme, the matching of objectives with resources and the establishment of an effective control system, have now been discussed. The third stage, the commercial exploitation of R & D output is, surprisingly, often the most neglected and therefore badly performed. Industry abounds with tales of new product ideas collecting dust on the shelves, of theoretical cost reduction opportunities never materialising in practice, of companies sitting on assets in the form of patents for products and processes for which they have no use and failing to realise their commercial value.

With some justice, it can be argued that R & D is about means not ends, and that it is the responsibility of other departments, marketing or production, to decide what use, if any, can be made of any particular piece of R & D work. It is difficult to resist the conclusion, however, that this line of argument betrays a defensive attitude far removed from the profit-orientated approach. At a minimum, the R & D department has a responsibility to ensure that decisions on the application or otherwise of their ideas are reached consciously, not by default. The more effective their participation in the decision-making process, the greater will be their sense of involvement and correspondingly their isolationism will diminish. In short, scientists should be expected to be businessmen.

Reference has been made to the need for 'conscious decisions' about the use of R & D output. The point can best be illustrated by examples of typically recurring situations:

## New Products

By definition new products offer, potentially at least, profitable growth opportunities. A company's ability to exploit them unaided will depend on the adequacy of its resources – financial, marketing and selling. If resources are not adequate as discussed in chapter 2, a number of alternative possibilities exist – seeking venture capital, forming a joint company with some other manufacturers with complementary skills, or merely licensing the idea and flourishing on the royalties derived from the hard work of others. Whatever market entry route is adopted, there is an overriding need to move quickly to gain maximum advantage from product exclusivity since, as Alvin Tofler so tellingly demonstrates,[1] technical lead times are shortening dramatically in all industries.

## Cost Reduction

Suppose R & D work led to the identification of potentially significant cost reductions for a particular product range, management may choose to reduce price with a view to gaining a more dominant share of that particular market. Alternatively, they may feel that the limited market growth prospects allied to the likely competitive over-reaction rules out what the Irish describe vividly as a 'retaliate first' approach. In these circumstances management might sensibly decide, government controls permitting, to use the higher margins and hence profits which the cost savings produce to help finance investment in some other business activity. Similarly, *product or process improvements*, whether or not patentable, represent assets which should be reliable in terms of increased market share.

## 'Discards'

The analysis of the value to the business of the output of any R & D department during a typical year is likely to show the normal distribution spread of a few outstanding successes, a majority of averagely useful projects, and a high proportion of 'failures'. On closer examination, these failures will invariably be found to include a depressingly lengthy catalogue of completed projects which for one reason or another have been judged inappropriate to the company's needs and therefore have not been adopted. These are wasting assets, the value of which is in many cases enhanced by the trappings – patents, trademarks, etc. Whatever one's views on patent law, it goes without saying that any company should seek the maximum possible legal protection of product assets (i.e. formulations), processes and brand names. However, there may be excellent competitive reasons why no attempt has been made in the past to sell discarded products to other companies, although it seems sensible to suggest that management should at the very least make an annual 'audit' to satisfy

[1]Alvin Tofler, *op. cit.*

itself that security rather than inertia is in fact the reason for stock-piling. Whether new products or discards, the common principle remains: always strive to maximise the commercial possibilities of R & D.

## CHECKLIST

- Why is the company considering an R & D programme?

- Is the management of the R & D department sufficiently strong to ensure that expenditure is controlled and that the output is utilised?

- Have clear objectives been set for the R & D programme?

- How frequently is research used or required?

- What was the R & D budget last year as a proportion of sales revenue?

- How does this compare with the expenditure levels of comparable firms in the industry?

- Does the R & D need to be carried out by the firm's own employees or can it be sub-contracted?

- Have suitable contract R & D companies been identified and evaluated?

- Have alternative methods of obtaining new products been investigated, e.g. licensing?

- What reporting systems exist to inform general management of progress on specific projects and the costs incurred?

- Is there adequate contact between those working on R & D and those responsible for using R & D output?

- Have steps been taken to ensure that developments not required by the company itself are nevertheless utilised?

- Do the employees of the R & D department appreciate that they are employed by a commercial organisation and not an academic institution?

- Is there scope for carrying out R & D jointly with firms with similar interests?

CHAPTER 4

# Test Marketing in the Low Budget Marketing Mix

BY RICHARD EASSIE

Test marketing is the research technique whereby a new product or service is put on sale in a small part of the country to analyse what happens when the product moves out of the protective arms of the company into the cold reality of the market place. Test marketing is the half-way house between in-company development and a full-scale product launch. The significant point is that it is the only type of research whereby the product is tested in a way which involves consumer purchasing in a normal shop situation without the public being aware that they are taking part in a research project. As with other types of research, test marketing is a means of avoiding wasted expenditure on products, services or even marketing tactics which have a low possibility of success. As such it is often an essential part of the low budget marketing mix.

## Characteristics of Test Marketing

The point of test marketing is the same as that of other kinds of customer research: to reduce the risks that are inherent in any new product launch. However, it differs from other types of research in a number of ways, the most important of which are:

- It is more costly in time and money than other forms of customer research.

- It is conducted in public where everybody, including one's competitors, can see what is going on.

- It is carried out in the market place rather than under 'laboratory' conditions.

With the increasing sophistication of attitude research, market segmentation studies, concept testing and other techniques it is not surprising that the death of test marketing is predicted with considerable regularity. Yet the technique continues to flourish, particularly where consumer goods are concerned. The reason for this must be that in many marketing people's view, the advantages of the third of the points listed above outweigh the undoubted disadvantages of the first and second points.

It would be worthwhile to look at each of these three points in rather more detail.

*Length and Cost of Test Marketing*

It seems likely that the cost of test marketing in terms of time is even more important than the cost in money. There are very considerable variations in the length of time allotted to test markets. A study of published data in Britain and the United States has identified successful new products which were on test for only six weeks at one end of the spectrum, and up to nearly four years at the other. In general, it seems that tests in the United States last longer than in Britain but, in both countries, the duration of test markets is getting shorter. There are several reasons for this. First, there is an increasing realisation that test markets cannot give absolutely accurate predictions of subsequent national marketing and that there is, therefore, no point in obtaining a very long series of readings. Second, there are the problems of security, and third, the improvements that have taken place in interpreting test results.

Nielsen data based on both Britain and the United States involving a study of 141 tests in consumer goods markets, shown in Figure 4.1., indicate that there is a very good chance of forecasting the final outcome of an eighteen-month test market after ten months. Within the sample there were only minor differences between toiletries, household and food products.

FIGURE 4.1.

*Build-up of Accurate Test Market Predictions*

| Length of Test | | Cumulative Percentage of Correct Predictions* |
|---|---|---|
| After | 2 months | 11 |
| | 4 months | 30 |
| | 6 months | 51 |
| | 8 months | 69 |
| | 10 months | 84 |
| | 12 months | 94 |
| | 14 months | 97 |
| | 16 months | 99 |
| | 18 months | 100 |

*Correct prediction is the forecast of the position after 18 months.
*Source:* Nielsen.

The rapid cumulative build-up of correct predictions shown in Figure 4.1. is noteworthy. It is, in fact, considerably better than the rate of learning found in other more scientific projects, such as the forecasts carried out at various stages during missile development programmes. The figures given are based on an analysis carried out in 1968. A later study by Nielsen covering thirty-four British brands in 1973 produced results very similar to those of the earlier work.

It is now general practice for tests to last between nine and eighteen months for repeat purchase consumer goods, though it is worth pointing out that a recent research programme found that 90 per cent of grocery buyers consider that they can decide whether a product has succeeded or failed in six months or less.

With regard to cost, one cannot produce any very meaningful 'typical' figures because there are so many variables, such as the size of the area, the advertising media used, the length of the test, the capital costs involved in production and so on. Excluding investment in plant, a total cost of £50,000 for a test market in a single television region is by no means unusual, but later in this chapter some suggestions will be put forward to show how the small company may keep its test market budget down to 20 per cent or even 10 per cent of this amount. It is also worth bearing in mind that in a test market the company is actually selling products so that, unlike other types of research, the test market brings in some revenue and although the profits will rarely be large enough to cover the extra organisational and research costs involved, they are still a help.

*Secrecy*

The second of the major drawbacks of test marketing is of the lack of secrecy: the exposure of one's plans and product to the competition. There can be no doubt that this is a danger, but it is probably one that is exaggerated. There are one or two well-known examples of front-runners in test markets being overtaken by rivals who have seen what is being tested and then gone straight into national distribution with their own product. Alberto-Culver used this approach to overtake Procter & Gamble in the United States anti-dandruff shampoo market when the latter were giving prolonged test marketing to their product 'Head and Shoulders'.

However, such situations are not very common. Unless a company indulges in long test markets or has a product that may be copied very easily, then the competition, if starting from scratch, has to be very agile to steal a march on the test-marketing company. Furthermore, such a competitor would be committed to taking a risk in going rapidly into national distribution that the original company thought to be unacceptable. In a study carried out recently for Mintel, 54 per cent of a sample drawn from Marketing Society members who had been connected with test market operations in the previous three years disagreed with the statement that 'the worst thing about a test market is that it lets the competition know what you are doing'; 14 per cent expressed no opinion, and 33 per cent agreed.

There are certainly cases where test marketing is not practical, but the secrecy factor is seldom the most important aspect.

*Realism*

'No amount of panel testing can beat the real world'. This remark by Victor Bonomo, the well-known American marketing man, sums up the great advantage that test marketing has over other research. It is, of course, possible and nearly always desirable to research different parts of the new product's marketing strategy long before one gets to the market place. Price, packaging, advertising copy and the product itself may all be tested, using well-established techniques, but each of these factors is tested in isolation and to some extent under artificial 'laboratory' conditions rather divorced from the real world.

As mentioned earlier, test marketing is basically different from all other forms of market research because it is most definitely something which happens in the real world, and is one of the few forms of market research in which the consumer is not aware that he or she is being studied. It is also the only stage in the product's market research programme where all the factors have to work together, rather than in isolation. It is quite possible to research any number of aspects of a marketing plan one by one and yet, even though each part of the plan seems satisfactory, one may still be uncertain as to whether they will all fit together. The final co-ordination of sales force, advertising, promotion, distribution and so much else can only be in the market place. In many cases this means test marketing, for just as test marketing may be more expensive and time consuming than other types of research, so national marketing normally involves far greater stakes both in money and reputation than those risked in a test market. There can be no more extravagant a form of 'research' than going straight into a national launch without having first done all that one can to obtain as clear as possible an idea of the likely outcome.

The realism of test marketing does not in any way destroy the value of pre-testing. Indeed this value is underlined by the expense and time involved in test marketing. Many methods may be used to improve the prospects of a product's success long before it gets to test market and the tendency is to increase the amount of research done before a product ever gets to the test market stage.

Pre-launch tests carried out comparatively cheaply and in private are necessary steps in any marketing plans. Nothing could be sillier than to go through an elaborate test market operation simply to find out something which could equally easily be discovered through a quota sample of five hundred people. But when a product has passed all the preliminary hurdles, then one is justified in going to test market as a final piece of research before undertaking the risks of a national launch, because test marketing is the only way of finding out whether a new product launch programme is really going to work.

**When to use Test Marketing**

It will have been noticed that most of the discussion of test marketing in this chapter has centred on consumer goods. Although the technique is certainly useful in some industrial markets, its main application is in the area of mass-produced consumer goods. Probably the major difference in marketing consumer and industrial products is that the former tend to be sold to a very large number of customers, often at the end of a long chain of distribution, each of whom may spend a few pounds or perhaps only a few pence on the product concerned. Purchases of industrial products, on the other hand, are often concentrated among a comparatively small number of buyers, frequently in direct touch with the manufacturers, and having substantial buying power. When one is in touch with a small number of reasonably well-informed customers there are usually easier ways of taking the temperature of the water than a full-scale test market.

There are also some technical problems that are likely to be faced in industrial test marketing. Industrial buyers may have their ears pretty close to the ground so that they will quickly become aware of a relevant test even if it is taking place in distant parts of the country. Purchasers from outside the test area may completely wreck the research readings if the true source of the sales cannot be pinned down. For these sorts of reason industrial test markets are much rarer than their consumer goods counterparts.

In general terms the value of a test market, because of its realistic assessment of the likely results of a national launch, has already been discussed. However, each product launch programme, consumer or industrial, must be judged on its own merits. In some cases, the need to exploit a fashion trend may mean that there is insufficient time available for a test market. In other instances, the product may need plant which precludes production on anything other than a massive scale so that it is impracticable to produce test market quantities. In general one must balance the risk and cost of immediate national launch against the time and cost of conducting a test market. This may be done by a systematic assessment of the probability of reaching certain sales levels and the calculation of the profit or loss positions arising from such sales, but it must be remembered that it may not only be the company's cash which is at risk in a national launch – prestige and reputation can also be involved and these too are safeguarded by test marketing.

Assuming that a test market has been decided upon then, in addition to a general look at the way the public reacts to the product, there are likely to be in each case some specific requirements, some particular aspects of the marketing plan which the launching company wants to examine with especial care and interest. Hopefully the test will seek to find out something more than whether the public likes the product, for a test market is not just a test of the product; indeed, it is not much of an exaggeration to say that test marketing should not be used to sort the good products from the bad, but to find out how to market products which are known to be good.

The test market is, in practice, likely to concentrate on one of three factors. The first is the accurate prediction of the sales likely to be achieved in national marketing; the second is closely related but sets out to see the relative effectiveness in matched areas of different marketing plans (such as varying levels of advertising and different promotions), and the third factor is where less concern is shown about the figures and more attention is paid to the trial run aspect of the launch, making sure that all the pieces in the programme mesh together as they should.

Most test markets should, therefore, be judged on their success in achieving one or more of these aims.

*Prediction of National Sales*

Much of the criticism which has been made of test marketing has resulted either directly or indirectly from incorrect forecasts of national sales. A brand in a test area obtains a market share of $x$ per cent after one year, then fails to reach a similar level after one year on the national market. The facile conclusion is that the test market was 'wrong'. Such conclusions are due both to the mistaken view that any test market area can be really typical of the whole country, and to the equally erroneous idea that the measurement of one factor, such as brand share, can give a picture of the whole operation.

No one area represents a microcosm of the country as a whole. There are so many variables that the chance of any town or television region representing an average for the entire country is so remote as to be not worth looking for. To begin with it is usually impossible to use the national press in a small area. Then there are variables in the demographic characteristics of the different areas, in income and employment levels, in urban and rural proportions, in the structure of the retail trade, in media watching and reading habits (not to mention overlap), consumption levels in the product field concerned, brand shares, the strengths of the company's own and the competition's sales forces. It can be seen that the list is virtually endless. Neither should the fact that marketing is about real people and that there are wide differences between the peoples of regions of any country, ever be forgotten.

This lack of typicality is not a cause for despair; rather it should be a matter for some joy that, in spite of the fact that no corner of a country is free from the uniforming influence of national television networks, the regions still manage to retain characteristics of their own. Nevertheless, some areas are obviously more typical than others. Equally, some parts of the country are more convenient in terms of media, sales force organisation, and so on. A systematic search will reveal which town or area is most suited to the purpose. The important point is not that the area should be typical but that it should be understood. If it is known how the area differs from the national picture then allowances for its peculiarities may be made weighting the results accordingly.

The experience of those who took part in the Mintel research showed that a wide variety of types of area had been used for test marketing. The results shown in Figure 4.2., including many multiple answers, refer to respondents' experience in the last three years.

FIGURE 4.2.

*Test Market Areas used in the United Kingdom*
*by Mintel Survey Respondents*

|  | Per cent |
|---|---|
| TV areas | 85 |
| Nielsen areas | 12 |
| Sales areas (not TV or Nielsen) | 50 |
| Town tests | 45 |
| Other areas | 15 |
| Shop panels/chains | 39 |
| Other/no answer | 11 |

*Source:* Mintel.

Respondents were also asked about the current trends in test areas (Figure 4.3.). In this case there were far fewer multiple responses and television areas came out as clear favourites, two-thirds believing that the trend was towards these areas.

FIGURE 4.3.

*Test Market Areas being used with Increasing Frequency*

|  | Per cent |
|---|---|
| TV areas | 62 |
| Nielsen areas | 3 |
| Sales areas (not TV or Nielsen) | 5 |
| Town tests | 17 |
| Other areas | 2 |
| Shop panels/chains | 23 |
| Other/no opinion | 14 |

*Source:* Mintel.

These survey results reflect the fact that the need to use test marketing is felt most keenly in the launch of repeat purchase consumer products backed by television advertising, a situation where the money at risk is large.

Experience has shown that there are considerable differences in the accuracy with which different types of data may be extended from test market results to successful national predictions. With regard to distribution it is often impossible to make more than the roughest assessment of national results since, whatever professions of help the retail trade may make, it is much harder to get shops to stock a product on test than one in general distribution. A 1970 survey revealed that one-third of grocers would not take test products.

With less than two-thirds of grocers willing to take a test market product even in theory it may readily be seen that any single new product will be likely to achieve a still lower level. Furthermore, the problems encountered in obtaining test market distribution are of quite a different type from those which face a product at the time of its national launch. Thus test market distribution figures can seldom be translated into predictions of what will later be achieved on a national scale.

Nevertheless, a factor such as the rate of repeat purchase is likely to show a strong correlation between test market and national results. In this instance the research is dealing with individual consumers and finding out whether, once they have bought the product, they will continue to think it worth buying it again.

An indication of the repeat purchase ratio is widely regarded as the most important yield of a test market but other aspects are also relevant, which brings us back to the question of understanding what is happening in the test market. It is not so much the final sales figures which tell the story; it is more the way in which these figures are constructed.

This means that a considerable amount of statistical work must be done on how the test market results are achieved. It is normal to start by constructing a model of what it is believed is going to happen in the test area and then comparing the results to see not only how they differ from the predictions but also where and why. This is most easily explained by means of the following example. A product is being launched into a test area with 8 per cent of the population, i.e. 1·4 million households. It is being sold at an average retail selling price of 20 pence per unit, and there are 10,000 potential retail outlets which might stock this new brand. The market's annual sales in the area come to £0.9m. a year which means £150,000 in each two-month period. Figures 4.4. and 4.5. show how the models of the likely, or hoped for, build-up of sales could be constructed.

The main point about the following tables is that they show how the final sales figures were obtained. Sales of a little over a million units could have been arrived at in many ways. A limited number of heavy buyers or a

FIGURE 4.4.

*Model of Retail Sales*

| 2-month period | Sterling Distribution | Sales per shop handling | Total Sales | Total Sales Units | Brand Share |
|---|---|---|---|---|---|
| | Per cent | £ | £ | £ | £ |
| 1 | 18 | — | — | — | — |
| 2 | 24 | 7·0 | 16,800 | 84,000 | 11·0 |
| 3 | 30 | 10·5 | 31,500 | 157,500 | 21·0 |
| 4 | 34 | 10·5 | 35,700 | 178,500 | 23·8 |
| 5 | 36 | 9·5 | 34,200 | 171,000 | 22·8 |
| 6 | 38 | 8·5 | 32,300 | 161,500 | 21·5 |
| 7 | 40 | 8·0 | 32,000 | 160,000 | 21·3 |
| 8 | 40 | 8·0 | 32,000 | 160,000 | 21·3 |

FIGURE 4.5.

*Model of Consumer Buying*

| Percentage Buying | Times Bought | Total Units |
|---|---|---|
| 36 | Once | 504,000 |
| 14 | Twice | 392,000 |
| 3 | Three times | 126,000 |
| 0·9 | Four times | 50,000 |
| | | 1,072,000 |

lot of people buying only one each; poor sales through many shops or weak distribution but excellent results through those shops which were handling the product; ineffective advertising seen by lots of consumers, or effective promotion seen by only a minority. All these opposite states of affairs could end up with the same results, though in practice, a knowledge of the statistical patterns common in one's market enable one to decide that some interpretations of the figures are much more probable than others.

Figure 4.5. shows that half the sales have gone to people who have bought only once in the sixteen-month test period, many of whom it may be presumed will not become regular buyers. On the other hand 16 per cent of sales have been accounted for by 3·9 per cent of the total number of households in the region. So it may readily be seen how vital it is to have a commentary on the whole test rather than to be satisfied with only the final score.

Even with a full model of test market results, it is often not possible to go straight to successful national sales and brand share predictions because of the probable atypical state of the test's distribution, promotions, etc. Nevertheless, the test market should have greatly improved the prospect of making worthwhile forecasts in a number of vital areas and thus considerably reduced the risks involved in a national launch.

*Area Comparisons*

It is sometimes considered desirable to test different marketing plans in separate areas. The problems of comparisons between areas are similar to those involved in going from area figures to national predictions. The analyst must be sure that he is comparing like with like, or else make due allowance for the dissimilarities between areas. In other words, he must be sure that any variations in the results from separate areas are due to the differences in the marketing campaigns being tried out in each, rather than differences inherent in the areas themselves.

The only other point that should be made is that since test marketing is a crude real-life tool, it is no good hoping that a comparison between two test areas will sort out the rival claims of very subtle differences in marketing approach. If, for example, the object were to test two levels of advertising support in different areas, then the difference in budgets must be substantial, say nearer 50 per cent than 5 per cent.

*Trial Run*

In addition to demonstrating probable sales levels, and just as important in many cases, there is a need to give product launch plans a trial run. A complicated scheme may seem to be fine on paper, but this is no guarantee of success in the market place. Will the sales force, the trade and the public behave in the way that has been forecast? Will the carefully designed timetable really be practical? Will the various aspects of selling-in, advertising, public relations and so forth mesh together in the way they are meant to? A complex programme may well urgently need a test run in a limited area before a national launch is risked.

**Keeping Costs Down**

From what has been said so far, it will be clear that a test market is a combination of a research operation and a dress rehearsal. It is the final stage of the development programme and, at the same time, the first step into the market place.

Test marketing cannot by its very nature ever be really cheap, but for the small company there are ways of reducing the cost well below what it would be if a lengthy test were to be carried out in a major television area, as will be shown in this section and those which follow.

To begin with, there is the question of how long the test should last.

To a considerable extent this depends on the frequency of repeat purchase. The pattern of behaviour will usually be much more quickly apparent in an item bought weekly than where the test is concerned with something bought only every two or three months. In general, as was demonstrated in Figure 4.1., it is seldom necessary to test products for more than a year. It is often useful and quite practical to take a decision on whether to go national after about nine months. This enables the tester to go into the national market just about a year after the start of the test market, which means that any seasonal factors affecting the test market are reproduced in the national campaign. So the first way of minimising costs is not to keep the test going too long. There is always the temptation to keep the test going for just one more month, to obtain just one more set of readings before taking the final decision. But unless everything is very much in the balance, such temptations ought to be resisted. The expenses of test marketing (small-scale production runs, market research costs, etc.) do not go down, instead they mount month by month. Neither will the test market, nor any other type of market research for that matter, ever give a totally certain result, so once the test has begun to produce a steady pattern of behaviour in the new product's sales and consumer reactions then a firm decision must be taken. This will save both time and money.

*Advertising Media*

For most consumer goods advertising is likely to be the major test market expense. The fundamental point to be made here is that the test market must use the same medium as is scheduled for use in the subsequent national campaign. For there is really no point in going into a test town using the local press if the national campaign is to be based on television.

It is easier to obtain a realistic test market using television than the press because there is only one commercial television channel, and for the viewer there is no way of knowing whether the commercials he or she is seeing are only being screened in their area, or are going out on the national network. On the other hand, a local paper, particularly a local weekly, can seldom be looked upon simply as a scaled down version of a national daily. Nevertheless, if it is intended to use the press in the national launch, there is no choice but to use the local press in the test.

As a general rule, it may be said that to use the local press in a test town will be cheaper than most television test campaigns, but television must be used in the test market if it is going to play the major role in the national launch.

*Test Area*

Assuming that television is in fact going to be used, the next question is what size of area is necessary, for clearly the smaller the area, the lower the outlay and the less money there is at risk. Equally obvious is the fact that the larger the area the more likely are the results to be in line with the national picture.

The ideal test television region is probably one containing 8–10 per cent of the country's population, hence the popularity in Britain of Southern and Harlech as test market areas. But testing in an area of this size is still going to be an expensive business, and the small company may well want to look for cheaper alternatives. Cutting costs nearly always has some effect on accuracy, but if a substantial saving may be made with only a slight loss of precision, then this may well be the best course of action for the small firm – and very often for the large company as well.

Providing that the company does not expect too much of the small test market area, it can be made to be a very serviceable tool. For instance, a great deal of data can be obtained from a test in a small area, such as Border, with 1 per cent of the national population, or with the even smaller Channel area with a mere fraction of 1 per cent. The scale of saving may be calculated from the fact that a 30-second peak time spot on Harlech costs £480, on Border £70 and in the Channel Islands only £12.

It is worth saying something more about Channel as a television test market area, for though the islands have some clear disadvantages they also have a number of strengths of great potential interest to the small company which wants to test a product with a minimum of risk.

It was suggested earlier on that a test market campaign was seldom a test of how well a company would do in obtaining national distribution since the test market distribution is often so difficult to obtain. It follows from this that some test markets where very low distribution is achieved may become more or less invalid because not enough consumers have been able to try the product, however desirable it may be, or however persuasive the advertising. In complete contrast, in Channel a company working in conjunction with the television contractor's sales experts is pretty well guaranteed 80 per cent distribution for any normal grocery product. Of course this is an artificial situation, but this does not matter if it means that the population has the chance to buy the product straight away, and that therefore initial purchase and repeat purchase data can be obtained much more quickly than when struggling to get distribution from mainland shops.

Some products, drink or automotive items for instance, are not suitable for the Channel area but for the small company with a limited budget and the need to try out television the Channel Islands should not be overlooked, as here a budget of £6,000 can buy a six-month test, including all research and advertising costs.

### Research

Market research will be discussed in detail in chapter 5, but as far as test marketing is concerned, it must be understood that it is the one area where the budget should not be trimmed. The whole purpose of test marketing is missed if steps are not taken to find out exactly what is happening in the market. The value of the prediction models is lost if there is no way of keeping a close check on whether reality is in step with the forecast results.

Most test markets need at least two types of research: a shop audit and a consumer survey. The shop audit will look at the sales of a product through different types of shop, the price it is being sold at, the effect it is having on rival brands, the relative sales of different sizes, flavouring, etc., and type of display it is obtaining. Company sales figures will reflect some of these facts, but the shop audit is very important since it reflects sales out of the shops whereas the company sales figures show sales into the shops, which may be two quite different pictures!

Because of the vital need for repeat purchase data, the best form of consumer information is often to be obtained from a consumer diary panel, in which a cross-section of the population fill in a weekly report on what they have bought. Many television companies have arrangements with market research firms whereby continuous panels are available on a syndicated basis. It is, of course, important that the panelists should report on a wide variety of products rather than just the one on test. This is both to see how competitors are doing and to avoid drawing the panelist's attention to the product which is being researched. For both the shop audit and the consumer panel it is necessary to start collecting data before the test launch so as to be able to obtain a 'before and after' view of the operation.

Sometimes it is also necessary to do other *ad hoc* research to find out specific facts about the test market. For instance, a random sample might be asked if they had tried the product, and if not whether this was because they had never heard of it, could not find it in the shop, or for any other reasons.

Research is an essential part of any proper test market. Unless it is carried out in a serious and professional manner it may not only fail to uncover what is happening in the test area, but may well prove even worse than useless, by providing false clues or painting too rosy or gloomy a picture, thus damaging future national launch plans.

### Some Further Hints

Before concluding, it is worth considering one or two other points. To begin with, there is the matter of the various types of 'laboratory' operation which have been set up with the idea of doing some or all of the task of the full-scale test market. It is not necessary to describe these operations in detail, but most of them work on the basis of an experimental shop, either permanent or mobile, where a sample of the public spend money on groceries after they have been exposed to a special showing of advertising material.

In practice, because of the absence of realism this type of research is not a substitute for test marketing nor do most of these systems claim to be substitutes. Rather, they are an extra stage in the research and, if a product passes their standards, it then goes on to a proper test market. From the viewpoint of a product launch on a small budget, there can seldom be any justification for the use of this type of research which is never cheap and which fails to eliminate the need for a test market.

In striving to make the test market like the final national launch it is important not to allow the test to have features which cannot be reproduced on a larger scale. More salesmen, better salesmen, priority deliveries or other privileged treatment are self-defeating in the long run. There are also subtler forms of special pressure which may upset results. For example, the mere knowledge that top management are interested in a test may produce quite uncharacteristic efforts from the area sales manager and his men. The fewer people who are aware that the test is indeed a piece of research, the truer the results are likely to be.

Another point which sometimes causes worries, is whether some popular test regions may not become over-tested, with the public in these parts of the country becoming atypical because of the excessive exposure to new products.

Fortunately, there seems to be no evidence that this is really a problem. In practice, even the most frequently used test areas do not become overburdened with new items. A check on the advertising of new products (both those on test and others) in the Southern Television area, one of the most widely used test markets, showed that only 3·4 per cent of all advertising air time was devoted to these lines. This was in spite of the fact that the research was carried out in the spring, the most popular time of year for new product launches. Although the marketing man who spends all his time worrying about new brands may be overwhelmed with their importance, the general public are not even likely to notice any rises or falls in the number of new items arriving in their local shops.

## Conclusion

Is it all worth it? Is the spending of so much time and money on a test market justified? Or is it a luxury which is reserved for companies with extravagant new product budgets? The answer must be that although there are exceptions, as has been mentioned earlier in this chapter, a test market should always be included in the marketing plans for a new consumer product unless there are decided reasons why it should be left out. The realism of the test market makes it a highly desirable instrument in the cutting down of risks. It is a piece of research which should be rejected as seldom as possible.

The final word should be left to two independent research resources. Nielsen, in a study of eighty brands' test markets in recent years, found that 45 per cent of them were withdrawn before national launch. Of course, some of these products might have succeeded nationally in spite of their test market performance, but it seems reasonable to suppose that most of them would have brought their companies more grief than glory had they not been test marketed but gone straight into national distribution. Of the 55 per cent of the brands which survived the test market, nine out of ten did well at the national level.

When one bears in mind that the companies studied by Nielsen are likely to have been of above average sophistication and to have spent a good deal of money on the earlier stages of product development and research, the failure rate in test marketing shows once more how different the real world may be from the neat theories of the planning department. For, as Nielsen pointed out, the manufacturers concerned must have thought their brands had a good chance of success or they would not have gone to the trouble of a test market in the first place.

## CHECKLIST

● Does the product lend itself to test marketing?

● What information is the test market seeking to obtain?

● What is the minimum length of test required to demonstrate the market potential for the product?

● Will the test region(s) chosen provide an adequate indication of national attitudes and sales?

● Do the test conditions accurately simulate those of the full-scale marketing effort?

● Is the test market being adequately monitored by research?

● Have steps been taken to ensure that the test market is not receiving special treatment which will distort the findings?

## CHAPTER 5

# Marketing Research on a Small Budget

BY CHRISTOPHER WEST

Information is the life blood of marketing. A marketing-orientated company requires a constant flow of varied information about the customers it serves, the suitability of its products, the services it should offer, the success or otherwise of various sales and promotion approaches and a number of more specialised problems. There are many ways of obtaining this information but market research is the only formalised approach widely adopted by marketing departments large and small.

This is not to say that a market research department or function is itself essential. A large number of highly profitable companies have been established and survived for many decades without their management seeing a market report or ever dreaming of commissioning one. In such situations market knowledge is either generated by the personal experience of the entrepreneur himself, or obtained by a process of trial and error during which the company locates a formula in market success.

With the ever-increasing complexity and competitiveness of the business environment both for industrial and consumer goods, it has become more difficult to comprehend all the forces which determine the success or failure of any product. Furthermore, the increasing specialisation of corporate management provides fewer executives with the rounded view of the business environment held by the traditional entrepreneur. Market research is a partial substitute for entrepreneurial skills and is a means of avoiding, or at least reducing, the wastage inherent in the trial and error system of market development.

Once a decision has been taken to use market research to provide a solution to a business problem there are many ways of increasing the cost-effectiveness of research personnel. These range from the identification of the correct problems to the choice of the specific research methods. This chapter sets out to show how a research budget can be minimised for any given marketing operation.

## The Role of Research in Marketing

Since most marketing decisions require information to support them, research of one type or another has a role to play across the entire spectrum of marketing activity. Leslie Roger[1] has summarised the most common research applications, but constant change in the business environment, coupled with the perfection of new research techniques, is continually opening new vistas for market research. The range of services which market research specialists are called on to provide now includes; the measurement of the current size of markets, estimating the market potential for new products, forecasting market trends, measuring product acceptance in the market place (product testing), defining and measuring the effectiveness of distribution systems, retail audits, searching for new products, planning diversification strategies, location and evaluation of acquisition candidates, probing attitudes, images, purchasing procedures and the factors which influence purchasing decisions, examination of the various sales and promotional methods which can be used to reach customers and monitoring their effectiveness, analysing the activities, strengths and weaknesses of competitive suppliers of products, and the identification and evaluation of government activity and legislation impacting on markets.

Most marketing research studies are composed of a combination of a number of the above functions though the precise emphasis tends to alter over time. In recent years the increasing availability of published market information has profoundly affected the subjects requiring research. Government surveys are now more detailed and more frequent and since the rules requiring companies to disclose information have been tightened it is generally easier to structure the activity in the market place. This enables the devotion of more time to the interpretation of the findings and has generally resulted in an improvement in the depth and quality of research.

There is also a fashion cycle evident in the uses of research, raising one type into prominence and causing the decline of others. The intensive use of motivational research in the 1950s declined when the themes became overworked. In the late 1960s corporate planning rose to a prominent position in the research world but is now waning, to be replaced by a growing enthusiasm for acquisition searches. Underlying all of these, however, providing the staple diet of the market researcher, is the fundamental analysis of the size and structure of markets, future trends and customers' purchasing practices and product requirements. This information is a basic input to all marketing strategies and the provision of it is likely to remain the main activity of the market research profession for some time to come.

[1]Leslie Roger, *Marketing in a Competitive Economy*, Associated Business Programmes (London, 1965), chapter 3.

All research buyers, and particularly those who do not have excess funds to spend at the byways rather than the highways of research, should remember that the ultimate objective of research should be to produce action. However sophisticated the research may be, it is a waste of money if it does not result in a document which states clearly the action which needs to be taken to profit from the conditions located in the market place. Clearly, in the final analysis, there has to be some compromise between what the market dictates and what the company can achieve with the resources at its disposal, but if marketing means anything at all the analysis of market conditions should precipitate the framing of a marketing strategy. There have been many occasions when research has been commissioned as a substitute for action – the fact that a study is in progress delays the evil day when action has to be taken. No company operating on a small marketing budget can afford this luxury and should keep a careful look out for the syndrome.

### Setting the Research Budget

Clearly the firm which embarks on research exercises in all the situations identified above will need to think in terms of a major budgetary expenditure, even though in the case of each individual assignment there may be methods of limiting the cost. Thus although there are many opportunities to use research, the small budget operator will need to confine himself to those areas where research generated information is *essential* rather than merely *useful*.

To determine how essential information is, it is necessary to examine the following factors:

- What is at risk as a result of the decision being taken?

- What is the degree of uncertainty surrounding the decision?

- What is the extent to which further information is expected to reduce uncertainty.[1]

The weighting of these factors will differ in various situations but clearly the more there is at stake and the more the risks can be reduced by sound information on the market the greater the justification for using research techniques. A multi-million pound investment in a new or little-known market would clearly justify a major research project by the manufacturer; conversely there should be relatively little enthusiasm for a project which will add little to the efficiency or earnings of the sponsor.

Although the research budget can be related quantitatively to the money at risk and the degree of uncertainty surrounding the decision[2] in theoreti-

[1]Matthews *et al*, *Marketing: An Introductory Analysis*, McGraw-Hill (New York, 1964).
[2]Institute for Quantitative Research in Economic Management Paper No. 19, Purdue University, *A Decision Model for Marketing Research Expenditure* (Lafayette, Indiana, 1963).

cal terms, each individual research sponsor will have his own idea on what the information is worth to him. This will invariably be related to the additional benefits he is hoping to accrue by having the information and, perhaps more simply, what it would cost him to obtain the information himself. To give an obvious example, if research is being undertaken to decide whether a new area representative should be appointed, the research bill should not exceed 50 per cent of the annual cost of employing the man since in six months he should prove his own worth. Unfortunately, relatively few firms are able to quantify the benefits they can expect to achieve from a research executive, and it is a common misconception that time spent by management obtaining market information is less expensive than hiring an additional employee to carry out the work, or to commission an outside organisation to do the job.

Research expenditure can range from a few hundred pounds to tens of thousands depending on the nature of the problem and the sophistication of the solution sought. What is not commonly appreciated is that the same problem can be examined from several different standpoints each of which has a different budgetary implication. There may in fact be a Rolls-Royce and a Mini solution to each problem, the difference being the amount of confidence that can be attached to the answer. This implies that the key to minimising research budgets lies in the objectives set and the research methods chosen.

## Research Objectives and their Budgetary Implications

As with other services, assuming that the research is properly conducted, the sponsor achieves a result which is commensurate with the budget he puts up. The first step in minimising the budget required is to ensure that the objectives to be achieved are minimised. This is a process which should occur in the earliest stages of a project, namely while the objectives for the research are being set. If research objectives are geared to a large budget then that is what will be spent and it is folly to think otherwise. The problem for most sponsors is that research acts like a drug; once taken successfully it is easy to become addicted and to demand increasing quantities before taking a decision.

In order to avoid excessive research it is important to recognise that much information is nice to have but not essential to support the business decision being taken. Typical temptations to be resisted are broadening the geographical coverage of the research when data for a single country would suffice at the outset; completing a depth analysis of all market sectors when only the priority areas are really important and demanding high degrees of accuracy when orders of magnitude are sufficient. All of these can increase the cost of research unnecessarily.

Setting the objectives and the parameters for a research exercise is a skilled task which should be undertaken only by those responsible for using the information to be obtained. A finely tuned exercise concentrating only on the essentials is infinitely more difficult to conceive and demands more pre-planning than one which covers every aspect of the problem. Such planning may itself be time-consuming but will pay dividends not only in minimising the research budget, but also in optimising the usefulness of the results.

The scale of any market research study is dependent on a number of variables which may be summarised as follows: information yield, product coverage, geographical coverage, accuracy and speed.

The information yield requested initially should be restricted to the absolute minimum since the quantity and type of information to be sought in a study is a primary determinant of cost. It will govern whether desk research will be sufficient to solve the problem or whether (more expensive) field research will also be necessary. Information yield will also indicate the scale of the field research required; in general to obtain greater detail requires more intensive research.

Although there are many situations where breadth of product coverage is essential for decision-taking, any limitations that *can* be placed on the number of products covered by the research can be a further help to minimise costs. There is a great temptation for research sponsors to request detailed information on every product variation. To do so can considerably escalate the research bill by increasing the number of applications or market sectors that require examination.

Over-dimensioning the geographical coverage is another costly trap that research sponsors can fall into. Unless an objective of the research is to guide geographical diversification by identifying the regions or countries offering the highest market and profit potential, there may be little point in demanding information for areas outside the territory served by the company. All marketing departments have limited resources and any information which is beyond the scope of those resources, whether nationally or internationally, is likely to be out of date before it can be used.

The accuracies demanded of the research findings can also be classified as a major budget escalator for research sponsors. Obviously no research sponsor wishes to purchase inaccurate information or to spend money on information that is only slightly more accurate than an informed guess. Only by providing accurate information can research reduce the risk inherent in all business decision-taking. However, what many fail to realise is that the levels of accuracy required can vary significantly between different situations and there is little point in paying for degrees of accuracy in excess of requirements. There are situations, political polls for example, where a few percentage points can determine whether the predictions are successful. In most business research assignments, however, accuracies of between plus or minus 5 per cent, or even 10 per cent, are quite adequate. Few markets, whether industrial or consumer, are sufficiently sensitive to marketing action to justify very high accuracies in the information base for the strategy developed. Indeed, there are many situations where an order of magnitude or even a qualitative measure (such as 'well in excess of £x million') are quite adequate for decision-making purposes. For a manufacturer considering a new market of which he hopes to obtain a 10 per cent share it is not particularly significant whether the total level of sales is £50 million or £60 million; what is important is that it is neither £5 million nor £100 million.

Any research assignment providing a high level of accuracy costs money; it increases the sample size and also the amount of time needed to conduct the analysis. To optimise the use of the research budget research sponsors should determine the level of accuracy which is acceptable in view of the decision being taken and the amount of money at risk, and demand no more from their research department.

Finally, many business decisions are finely timed and obtaining information quickly can be a vital requirement. However, speed can impose cost and other penalties on research which should not be incurred lightly. To achieve a rapid turn-round on one particular assignment the research department may have to displace other projects, employ a larger research team than the project really warrants, or forgo the benefits of using a research executive who has had previous experience in the market but is tied up on another project. Opportunities to share research costs and expenses with other assignments may be missed and a wasteful use of research techniques employed. This is particularly true in the case of multi-country research. The optimum method of carrying out multi-country research is to use a small team of researchers with the necessary language proficiencies and background experience, surveying each country sequentially. In this way the lessons learnt in each country are carried forward and the team climbs the learning curve only once. To complete the survey rapidly an obvious short cut is to use several teams researching each market simultaneously. In this case not only does each team climb the learning curve separately, thereby incurring separate learning costs, but travelling expenses may be duplicated and on completion of the project the results will require harmonisation – something which happens automatically with the single team approach.

High speed research has other dangers which may also have cost implications. The adage 'do you want it *quick* or *good?*' is often very true in research exercises and if in an attempt to meet over-tight deadlines quality is affected, the sponsor may ultimately pay a very high price in terms of the effects of using inaccurate information or the cost of redoing the survey. There are unavoidable lags in research exercises, such as the need to await the response from key information sources, and any attempt to circumvent these by using substitutes may seriously affect the quality of the findings. The analysis of research findings normally requires considered thought, and undue haste could interfere with this process to the extent that some aspects of the market are overlooked. Of course no self-respecting research executive will admit to this possibility but research sponsors must be sensitive to the dangers of working at high speed.

Having said all this, any research sponsor should seek to obtain the maximum information yield from the budget he is laying down. Although the project should be set up on the basis of minimum requirements there are often opportunities to squeeze additional information from the research techniques being employed and these should be not missed. Some published sources carry information on many varied aspects of problems which can all be gathered at marginal additional cost. Once the number and distribution of respondents has been agreed in the light of the agreed objectives, it may be possible to add questions to the checklist without distorting the research approach or increasing the cost. Once travel routines, either domestically or overseas, have been set, it may be possible to stretch them at marginal additional cost to cover more territory. Having given the research staff an indication of his minimum requirements and obtained a budget figure for the work, the research sponsor next seeks advice on how to optimise the information yield from that figure.

### Research Methods and the Research Budget

Consumer and industrial market research projects make use of a number of techniques which vary in their cost and the volume and quality of the information that they yield. Broadly speaking, the techniques which cost less to apply yield a lower volume or less accurate information. The reason for this is that the information yield bears a direct relationship to the time expended in obtaining it and high yielding techniques normally demand a heavy time input.

The major techniques employed by market research executives are, in ascending order of unit cost: desk research, postal questionnaires, telephone interviews, structured personal interviews, observation techniques, semi-structured personal interviews and depth personal interviews.

Each of the above techniques has specific advantages in terms of cost-effectiveness and efficiency of obtaining data. The major cost in all types of research is that of employing and maintaining personnel. Thus the costs incurred tend to increase in proportion to the length of time taken to perform each technique. The research buyer must also concern himself with the information yield from the techniques adopted. Rapid techniques may be low-cost but are still useless if they are unable to produce the data required.

### *Desk Research*

Desk research is an essential ingredient to most surveys to discover what has been said before on the subject and to prepare the ground for field research. It is particularly valuable where substantial published information relating to the market is available, as it is clearly wasteful to regenerate information already in existence. As previously indicated, published information on markets is becoming more plentiful from government, universities, trade and research associations and private sources such as publishers and industrial organisations. This should all be obtained, evaluated and collated before field research is undertaken. Although it is rare for desk research to provide a complete answer to any research problem, it may go a considerable way to providing background information for decision-taking. Even if this is not the case field research can help direct research by providing sample frames and lists of useful contacts which are essential for the proper conduct of the survey. A common weakness is for firms to overlook data already available in-house in the form of previous surveys, sales statistics, salesmen's reports and accumulated information within the marketing department. A major role of desk research should be to seek out this information and save field costs.

*Sales and Customer Analysis*

Research, like charity, should always begin at home. Sales records, even in the form of annual collections of invoices, provide a unique record of an organisation's contact with the market place. They may be analysed to provide such vital clues as distribution of sales by customer type, average order size, range of order size, relationship between product types ordered and types of customer, seasonal flows of orders, geographical pattern of business, distribution of sales between regular, repeat and new customers, and intervals at which customers place orders. This list is by no means exhaustive and serves only to indicate the wealth of information that often lies neglected in the files of companies large and small. If there is reason to believe that the activities of the company are typical of the business as a whole, then sales analysis will provide an important indication of market conditions and an input into the marketing strategy. Normally companies are in some way atypical and sales analysis will serve as a benchmark against which market opportunities can be assessed. Sales statistics become particularly interesting when they are compared with the global picture of the market place and reveal the strengths and weaknesses of the company.

*Sources of Ready-Made Market Information*

A finely developed nose for information sources outside the company can save a high proportion of research expenditure. A surprising amount of information on all types of market is available for no more than the cost of a phone call or a letter.

Over the last ten years published information on markets has improved immeasurably, both in terms of quality and quantity, a fact brought about

very largely by an increasing desire for governments to control and participate in all forms of economic activity. The major sources of information
in most countries are the government departments overlooking the various
types of economic activity and the index of Government publications
(published by HMSO) is essential equipment for all research staff. Trade
associations, international organisations, research organisations, the
national and trade press and university departments also have a variety
of interests in business affairs and all publish reports and research documents which may be of relevance for the analysis of a particular market
situation. Certain research companies, for example Audits of Great
Britain, collect large quantities of data on consumer markets on a regular
basis from sizeable panels of respondents. Generally more detailed than
Government statistics, this may be purchased on a 'per item' or contract
basis. Those developing marketing information should therefore familiarise
themselves with the relevant sources and establish a simple system whereby
information is made available or is channelled towards them with a
minimum of effort.[1]

No small budget market researcher should seek to collect and store all
information that might at some stage be useful. To do so would require
excessive space and incur heavy charges. It is therefore important to
collect sources on sources, i.e. those publications which index information
available. The *British Technology Index* published by the Library Association indexes technical articles in some four hundred journals while the
*Research Index*[2] indexes market, industry and economic data in approximately one hundred newspapers and journals. Even the smallest of firms
would expect to subscribe to the journals of immediate interest to their
business, but few will be able to cover all potential sources of information.
Subscriptions to the appropriate indexing services can overcome this
problem.

Having identified possible sources of information the next problem is to
physically obtain it. It is of course possible to purchase back numbers of
journals, but it is much cheaper to borrow them. Most business journals
can be loaned from the local libraries or from the National Lending
Library for Science and Technology at Boston Spa. Membership of the
Association of Special Libraries and Information Bureaux, (ASLIB) will
provide access to the specialist libraries run by companies and other
organisations, while researchers working in London have easy access
to such mines of information as the City Business Library, the Export

---

[1] A number of books cover the use of secondary sources. The reader may refer to D. E.
Davison, *Commercial Information—A Source Handbook*, Pergamon (London, 1963);
W. A. Bagley, *Facts and How to Find Them*, Pitman (London, 1962); R. J. P. Carey,
*Finding and Using Technical Information*, Edward Arnold (London, 1966); B. Houghton,
*Technical Information Services*, Bingley (London, 1967).
[2] Published twice monthly by Business Surveys Ltd.

FIGURE 5.1.

| Checklist of Important Business Information Sources in the United Kingdom | |
| --- | --- |
| International organisations | United Nations, Organisation for European Co-operation and Development, European Economic Community, International Monetary Fund, International Bank for Reconstruction and Development |
| Government departments | Trade, Industry, Employment, Building and Public Works, Customs and Excise, Commercial Officers at overseas embassies[1] |
| British Overseas Trade Board | |
| Foreign embassies (commercial departments) | |
| Foreign chambers of commerce | |
| Financial press | *Financial Times, The Times, Economist, Investors' Chronicle* |
| Trade press | see *Newspaper Press Directory*[2] |
| Trade and professional associations | see *Directory of British Associations*[3] |
| Government and industry research associations | see *Industrial Research in Britain*[4] |
| Political parties (research departments) | |
| Trades unions (research departments) | |
| ASLIB | |
| Commercial banks (research departments) | |
| Annual reports of public companies | |
| Trade directories | particularly *Kompass, Dun and Bradstreet* |
| Buyer's guides, exhibition guides and manufacturer's catalogues | |
| Classified telephone directories | |

[1]Check index of HMSO publications for specific documents.
[2]Published annually by Ernest Benn Ltd.
[3]Published annually by CBD Research Ltd.
[4]*Industrial Research in Britain*, Harrap (London, 1964).

Intelligence Library of the British Overseas Trade Board and the Patent Office Library.[5]

Information on the activities of most public and private companies is

[5]The last of these is particularly interesting for its extensive stock of trade and technical magazines.

available from their annual reports, which are either published or lodged at Companies House. The report most public companies provide is a fairly full description of their activities and although written for the purpose of impressing shareholders or satisfying the Company Registrar, these reports may provide clues on market conditions. The reports of private companies and wholly-owned subsidiaries usually give only the minimum financial information, but there are situations where this in itself is useful. Obtaining access to private company reports can be a time-consuming activity, particularly for those carrying out searches infrequently. For this reason it is best left to a specialist organisation such as Extel, who for a small fee will provide photocopies of the desired sets of accounts.

*Field Research Techniques*

Of the field research techniques, a mail questionnaire is usually the least costly method of obtaining data, and depth personal interviews the most expensive. This applies, however, when the techniques are measured in unit terms, i.e. the cost of one questionnaire compared with the cost of one interview. In fact, in terms of data yield personal interviews can prove the least expensive technique to apply as their productivity is far greater than alternative data gathering methods. It is impossible to generalise about the mix of techniques to be employed to provide a solution to any given problem. The optimum mix is dependent on a number of variables which may be summarised as follows: the size of the universe, the degree of concentration within the universe, the volume and type of information required from each respondent, the geographical distribution of the universe, the types of organisations or individuals to be contacted, e.g. manufacturing, distribution or service companies, housewives or heads of households, the status of the respondent being contacted, the availability of the respondent, and the speed with which the results must be made available.

The above factors dictate whether a broad-scale survey is required or whether a more limited, concentrated exercise will provide the information needed. If breadth is more important than depth then postal questionnaires or telephone interviews may be employed to conserve budget. If depth is of paramount importance then personal interviews will be necessary and a major objective in designing the study should be to keep the number of interviews to a minimum. The status and availability of the respondents indicates the timing and method of approach to respondents to be adopted. If heads of households are required then personal interviews can normally be conducted only at weekends or during the evenings. To avoid the high cost of such interviewing a mail questionnaire may be thought preferable.

## The Postal Questionnaire

Postal questionnaires can be a useful medium for asking carefully structured questions of a large sample of respondents. They are also useful as a means of contacting those whose availability either in their homes or offices is in some way restricted during normal working hours. The questionnaire permits respondents to reply in their own time or to channel the enquiry to another respondent. The postal survey comes into its own in certain types of consumer survey, particularly where contact is required with named respondents (drawn for example from customer lists) or where the survey sponsor has some leverage with respondents, e.g. as in the case with the Government enquiries.

The major disadvantage of the postal questionnaire is that the response rate can be poor, rarely more than 25 per cent in industrial surveys and possibly as low as 40 per cent in consumer surveys. The cost of the questionnaire approach must therefore be computed on the basis of the number of useful replies received, rather than the numbers sent out. The cost of designing, printing and dispatching questionnaires together with the necessary follow-up to encourage response can be considerable and there is now some evidence, at least in the industrial world, that falling response rates are beginning to bring the unit cost of questionnaires more into line with those of telephone interviews and even structured personal interviews carried out by a member of a field force.

The vagaries of response restricts the usefulness of postal questionnaires in situations where the structure of the sample is critical, i.e. where replies are required from specified numbers of certain types of respondent. Recognising this problem researchers have turned to the 'administered questionnaire' in order to combine the physical and cost advantages of the mail questionnaire with the persuasiveness of the telephone interview. In essence an administered questionnaire entails seeking the co-operation of a group of respondents by telephoning them and then sending the questionnaire by post. Experience has shown that the wastage through non-response is considerably lower than is the case with normal questionnaires (response rates of up to 90 per cent have been achieved even in industrial surveys), and because prior warning has been given the questionnaire can be both longer and more complex than those sent unsolicited.[1]

## Interviews

Interviewing of all types is the core of market research activity, but it is more time-consuming than other techniques and therefore relatively expensive. For this reason the interview programme is normally the key

---

[1]For further reference see Paul Erdon, *Professional Mail Surveys*, McGraw-Hill (New York, 1970).

determinant of the research budget and should therefore be the most closely scrutinised component of any survey being commissioned.

Interviews may be carried out either on the telephone or in person. In either case they may be structured or semi-structured; in other words, the questions to be asked can be completely formalised with provision only for predetermined answers (such as 'yes', 'no', 'don't know') or there may be some room for the respondent to frame his own wording of the replies. Personal interviews may also be carried out 'in depth', in which case the course of the interview is determined largely by the respondent and the interviewer has only a checklist of points that he wishes to cover during the discussion. An increasingly important variant on the depth interview both in consumer and industrial research is the group discussion, in which groups of respondents discuss the subject matter of the interview and can therefore take account of each other's comments. Structured interviews requiring the use of an interviewer may also be replaced by the panel of respondents who report on a regular basis using a diary or some other self-administered technique. In the case of television audience measurement surveys the information may be collected by a recording machine attached to a sample of televisions.

The budgetary distinction between these various interviewing techniques is the length of time they take to set up and complete. At one end of the spectrum a simple telephone interview can, in theory, be carried out in ten to fifteen minutes. However delays in obtaining the telephone connection, waiting for the operator to locate the respondent and recalling those who are absent when the first call is made, keeps the average striking rate of telephone interviews down to approximately seven per day. At the other extreme a depth industrial interview may take a day to carry out. As a rough guide, structured consumer interviews carried out in high streets can normally be completed at a rate of between twelve and twenty-five per interviewer per day, depending on whether a strict quota has to be filled. The most that industrial interviewers normally manage to achieve are two interviews per day. For rapid market appraisals, therefore, the telephone approach has a clear advantage both in terms of cost and time taken. For a more penetrating analysis it is necessary to employ personal interviews, and the cost and time penalties have to be borne.

The major time-consuming elements of personal interviewing are as follows: telephoning for appointments, travelling to the interview location, completing the interview, and writing up the results. Economies should be sought on all of these functions in order to minimise the research budget. The geographical grouping of interviews, the choice of interview location, the design of the interview checklist, the structure of the sample and the method of sample selection may also be studied and designed to minimise the time taken. The random walk interviewing technique, in which the sample of respondents is selected as the interviewer follows a random route through an area containing a concentration of suitable respondents, tackles several of the timing problems. Although widely used in consumer research, the random walk has somewhat limited application in the industrial sphere.

Clearly if interviewing is carried out by highly qualified research executives the cost will be high, whatever the striking rate. In some situations, particularly in industrial research, the quality of interviewing required is such that there is little alternative to using highly qualified interviewers, but in many instances, it is possible to employ specialist interviewers who work on a freelance basis. Most market research consultants either operate or have access to a field force of interviewers, and research departments within companies can also buy interviewing time. In many situations research or marketing managers may find that buying the interviews and carrying out their own analysis provides a cheaper solution to the problem than commissioning a full market study.

The principal task of those designing studies is to ensure that the balance of techniques is correct not only in terms of the information yield but also in terms of the cost to the client. Each movement up the techniques scale must be justified by the need to obtain less accessible or more precise data. Clearly there is no point in embarking on a field research programme if the information required is already published and desk research can seek it out. Equally, within the field research mix personal interviews should not be employed if telephone interviews or even a postal questionnaire will suffice.

**Phasing the Research**

In all surveys the sponsor must decide how much information he needs to solve his problem and the tolerances of accuracy that are permissible. Information needs have tended to polarise around the extremes represented by market appraisals and depth surveys. Market appraisals recognise the need for quickly assembled overviews of the market situation using small samples which are suitable as a basis for strategic decision-taking; depth surveys represent the normal full surveys for the development of product and marketing plans. Combinations of these extremes are becoming increasingly important as a method of reducing the budget commitment to research and providing breakpoints in surveys at which a 'go' or 'no-go' decision can be taken. This approach is most useful when firms are considering a large number of alternative new products or markets. In such cases there is little point in developing a substantial volume of data for each product or market when a rapid overview may indicate the existence of a 'no-go' situation, on the grounds of no customer acceptance, low sales volumes or low profit or growth potential.

The most common form of multiple phase study is that in which a first phase provides an overview of a large number of markets. The overview concentrates on obtaining the basic information required to rank the markets examined in order of attractiveness. The criteria used can be varied to suit the situation but might typically include current sales volumes, growth potential, the existence of any directly competitive products, prevailing price levels, the identity of other companies competing in the market and their profit records and preliminary customer reactions to the products. Quantitative information may be given as rounded estimates rather than precise figures, which providing the tolerances are similar on all data, should be sufficient for a ranking exercise. The overview is then used to select the priority markets which are sufficiently attractive to warrant an in-depth evaluation in the second phase of the survey. Products or markets rejected at the first stage screening may, of course, be held over for later examination if the priority markets prove abortive for any reason. The main virtue of the approach is that the research budget is concentrated on those sectors with the highest probability of achieving the objectives of the research sponsors.

The research approach need not be limited to two phases, it can be expanded to numerous stages, each considering a different aspect of the problem. One word of warning however; although multiple phase studies can result in cost savings, the constant 'stop-go' approach imposes certain cost penalties. More time is spent reporting results and there are fewer opportunities to economise on research techniques. For example, several recalls may be required to certain respondents to cover the different phases of the subject. Nevertheless, multiple phase studies are being successfully used to reduce budget commitments in cases where firms have many product or market options to examine.[1]

## Make or Buy

A key decision facing all marketing departments large and small, is whether to employ their own research staff or to make use of consultants. The problem is particularly difficult for those operating on a small budget since the addition of one member to the marketing team will probably represent a high proportion of annual expenditure. It is tempting to conclude that low budget marketing should always use consultant resources for research inputs, but the validity of the conclusion is dependent entirely on the nature and importance of the research needs, and the role that the research executive will play in the marketing team.

The principal criteria which all companies should examine in order to determine whether to sub-contract their research needs or employ their own research staff may be summarised as follows: the frequency and nature of information needs, the availability of personnel able to carry out the work internally, the speed at which data is required, the need for special research skills, the need for objective appraisals, and the nature of the markets being examined.

The use of multiple phase surveys for examining export markets is described in chapter 9.

In situations where there is a constant need for market data sufficient to keep one or more research staff fully employed or where the market research function can be combined with another in the marketing department, there is a strong case for retaining internal research skills. The advantages are that the researcher becomes fully conversant with the company and the markets it serves. This familiarity can make for an efficient research operation, providing it does not bias the results. However, not all problems can be handled by a small internal research team. In addition to the bunching of projects which inevitably occurs in all companies, there will often be a demand for research skills such as psychological interviewing and technical knowledge which are outside the scope of the small internal department. In both situations sub-contracting all or part of the research to a consultant is normally the most cost-effective way of obtaining the data.

The principal benefits which research consultants have to offer are as follows: the availability of instant manpower, guaranteed information for a fixed fee, cross-industry fertilisation, freedom from internal pressures and anonymity.

The principal advantage of the consultant to those marketing on a small budget is that he does not represent a continuing overhead and can, in fact, be switched on and off as required. For companies with sporadic research needs this is a major advantage which means that considerable cost savings can be made by using consultant services. Perhaps of greater significance, however, is that most consultants offer a guaranteed information yield for a fixed fee estimated in advance, whereas the firm which operates its own research department has in effect established an open-ended commitment. At the best of times research is difficult to control and when mixed with other activities within the company it is often some time before it is possible to ascertain whether value for money is being obtained. Proposals sought from consultants state explicitly what data will be generated for the fee being charged.

Although there are advantages in specialisation it does carry the disadvantage that the research may become conditioned by the accepted folklore of the industry and therefore produce biased results. Some consultancies also permit cross-fertilisation of ideas from one industry sector to another. Examples of this abound in terms of a transposition of marketing approaches used in the consumer markets into industrial marketing product-marketing techniques for services.

Internal pressures are a problem in all companies and are likely to be particularly strong in small companies where the personnel form a closely-knit unit. In these situations an external research consultant can be particularly valuable since the answers he provides can be seen by all to be free of the vested interests within the company. Many research documents are used for political purposes within the companies, but to be valuable in this role they must be seen to come from an unbiased source if the expenditure on producing the report is not to be wasted. Similarly when the field work is being conducted there is strong risk of biased results if the identity of the research sponsor is known. Indeed, in some situations it is imperative that the sponsor remain anonymous for commercial reasons. The consultant can offer this anonymity and guarantee that the results of the survey remain confidential.

## Salesmen for Research

A good salesman is inevitably an important source of marketing information but there is a strong temptation to make him the only source in companies carrying out their marketing programmes on a small budget. Even in more elaborate organisations there is a tendency to regard the market development programme carried out by members of the sales team as an alternative to marketing research. At first sight the argument can be persuasive; first-hand experience by sales personnel is obviously preferable to the second-hand (some would say vicarious) experience provided by a market research report. No market research executive, so the argument goes on, can understand the product as well or be as positively committed as a salesman, and it is therefore unlikely that he will correctly interpret the market situation. Finally, the sooner a new venture is revenue-earning, the better for all concerned, and research serves only to delay this happy day.

To accept these arguments is to fail to understand the true purpose of research, which is not to sell products but to pave the way for the development and implementation of a marketing strategy. In fact, the outcome of a research programme may be a decision not to enter a market since it may be shown that to do so will result only in losses. The information derived from a market research survey and that from salesmen's reports are complementary rather than competitive and while information from the sales force is an essential input to all marketing strategies, any exclusive dependence on this source of information has a number of severe disadvantages.

First, the salesman attempting to complete a checklist of questions during his calls risks exposing himself as a novice at a time when he should be projecting an image of competence, persuading customers and distributors that he understands their requirements. Second, the qualities required of a good salesman, such as drive and commitment to his product, are hardly appropriate for an unbiased and critical appraisal of market conditions. The nature of the commercial relationship between the salesman and his customer may also lead to distortions in the information passed over. Finally, using salesmen to gather the information on which a marketing strategy is to be based implies entering the market before the strategy is defined. This is obviously possible in some circumstances but in the majority of cases is likely to be wasteful of marketing resources. The decisions which arise out of a marketing research programme should ideally be taken *before* a salesman sets foot in the territory.

## Joint Research

Many marketing problems are common to a large number of companies and in both industrial and consumer markets the sources of market information are also shared. While this is more true of consumer than industrial markets, both types of research consultant have developed research approaches which enable their clients to share the cost of a research programme with others who either require the same information or who need questions asked of the same respondent. The two types of research which all companies operating on a small budget should be aware of are the *multi-client* (or syndicated) research survey and the *omnibus* survey. Both types of survey tend to depend on the initiative of the research consultancies for their establishment, though it is not unknown for groups of companies to join together for the purpose of commissioning a survey. This may be done under the auspices of the trade association which distributes the information to all its members, and any company which considers that there is likely to be a widespread demand for the information which it is seeking and does not object to sharing it with the remainder of the industry should consider the idea of pressing for their trade association to commission the research.[1]

### Multi-client Surveys

The concept of the multi-client survey is that the cost of a complete research programme which has defined objectives is shared between a number of companies. In most cases the cost per subscriber is set in advance together with a minimum number of clients for the survey to proceed. Each client receives the full output of the research programme though there may be some scope for tailoring the results to the individual requirements of subscribers. Subscriptions range from a few hundred to several thousand pounds depending on the scope of the research and the degree of exclusivity that is agreed in advance, but in all cases the individual subscriber receives many times the value of his fee in terms of research output.

The multi-client approach is more common in North America than in Europe and many of the leading consultancies have libraries of reports providing basic market data on a wide range of products and emergent technologies. Though often insufficiently detailed for tactical decision-

---

[1] In the case of export studies there is in addition a Government grant scheme which covers 30% –50% of research costs. This is administered by the British Overseas Trade Board. See also chapter 9 ('Exporting on a Small Budget').

making, such reports can lay an adequate basis for planning and enable any subsequent research to concentrate on the finer marketing points.

There is a 'take it or leave it' atmosphere about multi-client surveys which does not appeal to all research buyers. There is also inevitably an element of wastage since in order to satisfy as many sponsors as possible the consultant will endeavour to produce a broad spectrum of information, not all of which will be useful to every client. However, since such surveys are sold on the basis of a proposal or prospectus which sets out the information to be sought in the course of the survey, each client does have the opportunity of estimating what proportion of the yield is going to be of value to him, and how cost-effective the expenditure is likely to be.

*Omnibus Surveys*

The omnibus survey is motivated by the same objective as the multi-client survey, namely to share the cost of the research programme, but is conceptually different and potentially more useful to the individual client. Whereas the multi-client survey builds on the shared information needs of sponsors, the omnibus survey recognises that companies share customers and therefore need to ask the same people different questions. In the multi-client survey both the research programme and the findings are shared, in the omnibus survey only the research programme is shared. However, since in any survey the greatest costs are incurred in setting up the interview programme and the marginal cost of asking additional questions is relatively low, omnibus surveys represent an inexpensive method of obtaining answers to questions. For as little as £60–£70 companies can question samples of a thousand adults.

The normal method of charging for omnibus research is on a 'per question' basis. Charging rates vary according to whether the question is structured or unstructured, which affects the difficulty of analysing the results, and quantity discounts may be given. Costs also include computer analysis and the client receives a printed tabulation of the results, together with details on the size and structure of the sample contacted.

The omnibus approach is ideally suited to the research situation in which answers are required to relatively few questions and therefore the cost of mounting a full survey is likely to be prohibitively high. Depending on the charging rates of the consultants there is obviously a cross-over point at which the omnibus approach ceases to be a viable proposition and a specially mounted *ad hoc* survey becomes worthwhile. There are no hard and fast rules on this and although it is unusual for a client to place more than ten to fifteen questions on an omnibus survey each research case should be evaluated on its merits. The length of an omnibus questionnaire is dictated by the amount of time the interviewer can hold the respondent's attention. This is usually about one hour and those running the omnibus tend to limit each sponsor to fifteen minutes of questions. However, a high proportion of omnibus users ask only two to five questions.

Omnibus research is currently applied almost exclusively to consumer markets mainly because the homogeneity of the market place lends it to this type of approach. The greater fragmentation of industrial markets means that there are fewer companies interested in each segment and the service is therefore less likely to be used. There are, nevertheless, some categories of industrial respondent who are in frequent demand as a source of information (such as architects, doctors, veterinary surgeons and farmers) and a form of omnibus has been developed to research their requirements. The major problem to be overcome is that such respondents are insufficiently numerous for a fresh sample to be constructed for each survey. There is, therefore, a problem of continuous intrusions into the same respondent's time. To avoid this, *panels* of respondents who agree to make themselves available have been established to answer questions on relevant subjects at regular interviews. The panel is then made available to research sponsors as required, but costs are shared only if two or more respondents wish to use the panel at the same time. The savings arise because of reduced time taken to set up interviews and persuade respondents to co-operate.

Consumer omnibus surveys are run at regular intervals, depending on requirements, and are aimed at the most frequently used samples of respondents. Most consultancies specialising in this type of research run a general sample and a number of specialist groups such as motorists, housewives, and teenagers. Parallel services are available in other European countries and the larger research companies with overseas connections can offer a European-wide service. The construction of a list of suitable omnibus surveys, their frequencies and their charges should be a priority task of all small budget market researchers.

### Control of Research Expenditure

There is a tendency to feel that once a market survey has been set up with an agreed coverage and research approach that all budgetary considerations are over. True, in the case of those using consultants the fee may have been fixed and should not change irrespective of the inputs the consultant may have to make but even then there are problems which can arise which will lead to sponsors' getting less than full value from their investment and even force them to commit further expenditure. Research is one of the most creative of business functions and as such it can prove extremely difficult to control. There are many variables which have to be taken account of during the actual performance of a survey, relating to such factors as the respondents yielding the information, the way in which the techniques are deployed and the personal qualities of the research staff themselves. All research sponsors should closely monitor the progress of surveys if budget overrun or waste is to be avoided.

The major budget-wasting problems which can occur during market surveys are: inefficient application of the techniques chosen, slow progress of the survey, failure to meet key respondents and incomplete coverage of the questions asked. All of these may cause the survey to take longer than scheduled. Any inaccuracies in the findings may cause further losses if marketing action is based on them.

The source of the problems may lie in the market place or in the research department itself. Some respondents are difficult to meet, some questions cannot be answered, machines, particularly computers, do break down. The small budget research sponsor cannot be expected to control all such events; having paid his specialist he is hardly about to do his job for him, and he rightly expects the specialist to come up with the solutions. However, it is worth remembering that the biggest cost in research is the payment of professional time and there are some simple steps which can be taken, even by those who know nothing about research, to ensure that the time for which they are paying is profitably employed:

- Provide the research staff with *all* the information you can on the market under review; this saves them spending your money looking for what you already have.

- Insist on regular meetings with the research staff – not the departmental manager, but those actually working on the projects, have them explain the progress of the survey and check this against the pattern set out in the research design.

- At each meeting ask the researchers to summarise findings to date and draw conclusions. They won't necessarily be accurate at the early stages of the project but will show whether the staff are getting a feel for the market.

- As far as possible check findings against your own experience. You may not be right, but justifying their case exposes the depth of knowledge of the research staff.

- Be prepared to accept draft reports and oral presentations of findings if the information is required quickly; let the final report follow in the fullness of time.

- Have your final question and answer sessions with the research staff as soon after you have read the report as possible, while the survey is still fresh in their minds.

All clients can make positive contributions to their own surveys, not the least important of which is ensuring that the research staff know the true purpose of the survey, and letting them feel that the information they are producing is not only useful but is in fact going to be used. A sense of importance and urgency will keep research staff on their toes; inefficiency and tardiness are more likely to occur in a relaxed atmosphere. If urgent action based on the research findings can be taken during the survey then so much the better.

Finally, it is worth remembering that there is only one truth, even though it may appear in many guises. There is a temptation to judge the value of a market survey by the newness of the findings and the sense of shock produced. If the research sponsor has any knowledge of the market this effect may be difficult to produce and many appear to feel that they have paid to be told what they already knew. If they are *confident* that this is so then they should ask themselves why they sponsored the research in the first place.

## CHECKLIST

- How much information exists within the company on the size and structure of the market for its products, future demand trends and the requirements of customers?

- What are the objectives of the research programme and are these the minimum necessary for decision-making?

- How much is at risk in the event of the wrong decision being taken?

- What is the minimum geographical coverage of the research that is acceptable?

- What levels of accuracy are acceptable?

- Has the product coverage been minimised?

- Can the timing of the research be scheduled so as to minimise expenses?

- Are the research techniques being used commensurate with the objectives and is maximum use being made of the lowest cost techniques?

- Have published sources of information and internal records been examined thoroughly for relevant data?

- Can the research effort be phased so that money is not wasted on examining unproductive market areas?

- Does the volume of research work justify the maintenance of a permanent 'in-house' research team?

● Have suitable research consultants been identified and evaluated?

● Is it possible to make use of syndicated research?

● Is there sufficient liaison between marketing management and research personnel to ensure that projects yield the information required and that valuable experience gained in the market place is not lost?

# CHAPTER 6

# Public Relations on a Small Budget

BY NORMAN HART

The successful operation of any commercial organisation depends very largely on its maintaining good relationships with numerous groups of people, usually referred to as its 'public'.[1] Such good relationships may be established and improved without much thought being given to the matter, or they may result from a carefully planned and continuous programme. Increasingly, businesses both large and small are finding that some element of planning is necessary in all their operations in order to utilise fully the skills and techniques which are becoming available to modern management to improve efficiency and match up to competition. Public relations is equally amenable to planning.

The 'PR universe' (Figure 6.1.) shows that certain specific public sectors impinge upon a company's activities, and that the company has a dual role, that of a transmitter and receiver of information. Messages are being formulated at the nucleus of the universe, and transmitted to the satellite sectors in such a way as to ensure good reception. Subsequently there is need for feedback in the way of a response to the messages, and the feedback will in turn determine the nature of future transmissions.

The five essential ingredients to effective public relations activity are:

- Define the company's PR objectives.

- Determine the publics which are to be influenced, i.e. the precise target audiences.

- Decide what messages to transmit and why.

- Establish the most effective means of communicating the message, i.e. the channel of communication.

- Build in a feedback system, i.e. a means of listening to the audience's point of view.

[1] J. W. Riley, ed., *The Corporation and its Publics*, Wiley (New York, 1963).

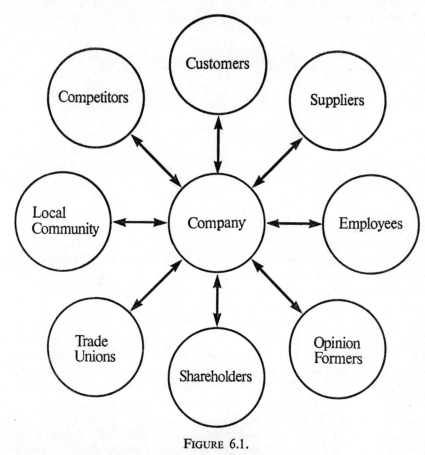

FIGURE 6.1.

*The PR Universe*

The similarity between the above five features for a public relations activity and those which are laid down for a marketing plan or indeed an advertising campaign, should be noted. It is important to do so since in essence a similar process is being followed: the difference is in objectives, in time-scale and sometimes in techniques. In the case of public relations the objectives will cover a far broader group of publics, and the gestation period will usually be much greater. An industrial dispute, for instance, will not usually be resolved by the public relations department of a company but rather by personnel management in conjunction with line management. The public relations function here is more concerned with the conscious effort over a long period of time to build up good relationships with employees in such a way that there is a climate of mutual trust and respect which will help to avoid an industrial dispute taking place. A similar process is involved in recruiting employees from the local community or in building a strong and attractive reputation amongst investors. Public relations then, is more a strategic tool of management than a tactical one, and this in turn underlines the need for careful planning.

**Setting Objectives**

Whilst many public relations activities will be concerned with publics other than those who have a direct influence on the purchasing process and the market for the company's products, it is as well to realise that publics are often inter-related and that even whilst here the consideration is primarily that of contributing to the marketing effort, there will be a spin-off which is valuable in other aspects of a company's activities. Public relations can only be an effective weapon in the marketing armoury if it is integrated with both corporate objectives and more particularly with the marketing plan. It must take upon itself the role of producing a favourable climate of opinion amongst potential buyers which will provide a sound base from which to launch the highly intensive advertising, sales promotion and selling activities, enabling them to reach a successful conclusion with the least effort and at minimum expense. Much of the scepticism or indifference amongst management towards public relations activities is due to the absence of specific goals which can be seen to be worthwhile in simple business or profit terms. Anyway, why not? For if there is no evident value in an activity, surely there is little point in conducting it. The dividing line between public relations and other forms of promotion in the marketing mix is hard to draw and will vary from one company to another. Nevertheless the following typical selection of objectives will serve as examples of what can reasonably be set as public relations objectives.

- To produce recognition of the company's position in the hierarchy of suppliers.

- To secure a reputation for a company's products as being good value for money (or safe, or strong, or accurate).

- To make known a new brand name such that one in two buyers automatically associates it with the right product and company.

- To ensure that 80 per cent of potential buyers relate the company name to the products it supplies.

- To cause all buyers to form an opinion that the company is honest, fair, ethical, and generally one with which they would like to do business.

- To exert influence on parliament to give tax concessions or other special benefits to the company's own group of products.

- To bring to the attention of Government, and to exert public pressure about, the 'dumping' of products which are directly competitive.

- To enhance the reputation of the company's own staff amongst journalists, opinion-formers and customers so as to build up confidence in the company itself.

A notable omission from the above list of examples is 'to obtain free editorial publicity about a new product and to obtain enquiries'. It is arguable whether this is public relations, though clearly such 'press relations' activities have a most important role in a company's operations. Reference is made later to editorial publicity for products though it might more properly be placed in the category of sales promotion. So far, little has been said about public relations 'on a small budget'. In the sections which follow, emphasis will be laid on the practical do-it-yourself approach, rather than on advanced, albeit highly professional techniques, which may be very expensive. Let there be no mistake about public relations and cost. It is emphatically not a cheap or free form of publicity which can be used in place of advertising. Many of the techniques are certainly not cheap, and as will have been seen, the function is rather to support and complement advertising and selling than to replace it.

### Definition of Publics

Earlier it was pointed out that a common failing in public relations is in the setting of precise objectives. A second failing is often in omitting to define the public or audience to which a message should be addressed.

If work is to be done 'on a small budget' then it is vital that it be done efficiently or the effect may not be achieved. For maximum impact not only must the purpose be defined, but the exact group of people must be listed in order that the most effective channel of communications is used. Contrast, for instance, the difference between influencing a national airline to purchase a new aircraft with influencing that same airline to use a particular brand of coffee sachets. Now consider the differences in publics if selling the same coffee to housewives, or alternatively to the canteens of industrial companies. To complete the circle, consider selling a new aircraft to industrial companies for their own use. In each case, not only do the number of potential buyers vary considerably, maybe from a dozen or so to twenty million, but also there are variations in their social status, location, age, sex and indeed in their position to make a judgement.

For a commercial company engaged in selling goods or services, the market can be broken down into what are popularly referred to as consumer and industrial publics, the latter including manufacturing and service industries, commerce and institutions such as hospitals and educational establishments. The supply channels between these two publics are different: the industrial public consists of the supplier being in direct contact with its customers, whereas in the case of the consumer public, goods leaving the supplier pass through distributive and retail channels before reaching the customer. In the case of consumer publics the pattern of distribution and influence is clear-cut, with the customer usually having the sole authority to make a decision. Sometimes there is a split in the decision-making process, for example both a husband and wife may have a point of view on what television set to purchase; but with breakfast cereals, the children might exert the strongest influence. Most times, however, the choice of purchase rests with one person. For instance, a man will choose his own beer, newspaper, tools, cigarettes; a woman her own stockings, hand cream, detergent, magazine, baker; a child, perhaps ice-cream, comics and sweets.

Each product market can usually be broken down into segments. For instance, a particular talcum powder can be shown to have appeal to, or to satisfy a need for certain well-defined categories of people, for example, women in higher income groups, over the age of forty and predominantly in the south of England. Others will be suitable for babies, or for men. Clearly, the media to be used to convey a message to one group is likely to be different from that to another. The message, and its style of presentation, will also be different, even for the same product.

Whilst the pattern of distribution is always changing, with the retailer having a decreasing role in the process of persuasion, there are still many products, especially in consumer durables, where his function is important. Even if retailers do not exert an influence in themselves, they still need to be convinced that they should stock a particular brand. Similarly with wholesalers, stockists, and other people in the distribution chain. Here, the media used in connection with the ultimate consumer will have a major effect, but to this can be added a whole new range, such as trade press, exhibitions, and conferences.

Some of the forces which can be brought to bear on a prospective customer include; the sales force, press advertising, all kinds of literature including editorial news, feature articles, and house magazines, films, public events and special functions.

With industrial marketing the pattern of influence is often far from clear. A 'decision-making unit' may well comprise a dozen or more people within one company.[1] For major purchases there may be engineers responsible for laying down the specification for precision and speed, production controllers to comment on the functional aspects, accountants on both capital and operating costs, buyers on delivery dates and competitiveness of quotations, and the board, maybe, from a point of view of profit. Again, each product market can be segmented for instance into industry

[1] *How British Industry Buys*, Hutchinson (London, 1966). Gordon Brand, *The Industrial Buying Decision*, Associated Business Programmes (London, 1972).

groupings, into size of company or geographical location. Within each purchasing unit, however, the groupings are quite complex and, clearly, media which will reach out to managing directors may differ from that to scientific advisers or purchasing officers. Furthermore, the nature of the message needs to be tailored to the type of person to which it is addressed. Clearly, a public relations exercise cannot hope to be effective unless first the publics are defined accurately. Maybe in a given instance this represents no problem. Usually, as has been indicated, there is some complexity and variety amongst a company's customers, and market research may be required to define the audience and the message required to influence their decisions.[1]

**Channels of Communication and Media**

It is intended here to examine six major means of communication, laying stress on how each may be used with a minimum of expense. Some are fundamentally more expensive than others, for example, press advertising as against editorial publicity (or a pleasant telephone manner), and this leads to the need, finally, for an efficient combination of activities, which can be referred to as the PR mix.

*Publications*

A particularly valuable feature of publications in public relations is that they are of a more permanent nature than most other vehicles of communication. This is especially true of *brochures* and *booklets* which might be produced to put across the nature of a manufacturing process, the care and precision which is put into a product, the amount of effort invested in research and development, or the extent to which a product contributes to the welfare of the community. The design and presentation of printed matter must of course reflect the image of the organisation, and for this reason the temptation to economise falsely should be resisted. However, certain basic rules can be applied to keep within a relatively small budget.

The first step is to avoid wastage in re-writes and re-designs by setting about the whole production process in a methodical manner. The objectives need to be defined and an outline produced before setting about writing the copy. A designer should be brought in only after the copy has been agreed, and then a tight briefing is necessary so that the objectives and constraints are known in advance. High quality, if this is required, can be achieved without high expense. Careful and restricted use of colour, avoidance of complex artwork, detailed attention to the type make-up, and a good production run can do much to reduce the unit cost of a publication. With the advances in offset lithography it is sometimes acceptable to use even electric typewriting in place of the more expensive typesetting. It is important to realise that multi-coloured glossy brochures can backfire in public relations terms. They can be indicative of a company

[1]N. A. Hart, *Industrial Publicity*, Associated Business Programmes (London, 1971).

with rather more money than sense as against a simple workmanlike publication which, if professionally produced, can create a favourable, and certainly acceptable, connotation.

*External house magazines* often have an important role to play in maintaining a regular flow of information about a company and its products to key audiences. This is particularly so with industrial products where there tends to be a good deal of innovation and the number of potential buyers is small. It also applies in consumer marketing where it can forge a valuable link with distributors. The editorial content needs careful consideration to ensure that it is directly relevant to the job in hand. When house magazines resort to cooking recipes and hints on hobbies, or births, deaths and marriages, then it is time to have a reappraisal. The latter items are, of course, quite valid for an internal magazine intended for employees, but only rarely can an internal and external house magazine be combined successfully into one. As regards production, the temptation to emulate the class of trade and technical press must be avoided if budgets are to be kept down. Many very successful company periodicals are no more than what might be described as duplicated broadsheets. Yet they do a first-class job. Customers are usually far more interested in content than in presentation, and the overriding factor is to put across the points succinctly without verbiage. It might be said, with some justification, of house magazines that large sums of money are often spent producing over-lavish and enlarged publications which, as a result, do not receive the attention a much simpler format would obtain. Regular communications in printed form are valuable. It is often most acceptable for these to be in the form of a simple unpretentious news-sheet costing around fifty pounds for a thousand copies or so.

The *Annual Report* is a useful opportunity for correctly positioning a company in the eyes of its customers, for it is certainly read by a wider audience than shareholders. The past decade or so has seen a good deal of change in the presentation of annual reports starting from the stark financial document required by law, and developing into a highly colourful and descriptive booklet that is as impressive as it is expensive. The fact is that designers are every bit as able to produce an inexpensive annual report as they are something which is lavish. If the opportunity is going to be taken of supplementing the statutory statistics, then for instance some facts about the company's progress and the interesting developments in products and distribution can be added. This can be done both professionally and economically. It may be fair to argue that since a printing job has to be done anyway, it might as well be made to work for its keep by including an interesting editorial content and, indeed, by having an inexpensive run-on which can be distributed to customers.[1]

[1]Joan Nicholson, 'Why Annual Reports Misfire', *Management Today* (London, January 1972).

*Sponsored books* are a little-used public relations tool, and that alone is a good reason for considering them. Many leading book publishers are very keen to examine opportunities for a book about a specialised subject that in itself might not be profitable in book trade terms, but with a suitable sponsor can be turned into a self-liquidating operation. A 'history of the company' is unlikely to fall into this category, but 'craft uses of cardboard' may well find a wide market and do much to improve the image of a very mundane product and at the same time give prominence to the company (a boardmaker or a converter) sponsoring it. There is after all something very prestigious about being associated with a book, and the writing of it can often be undertaken, or at least guided, by a staff man. Given the right subject angle and a market of a few thousand readers, the net cost can be very low.

As education moves away from the purely academic to encompass more matters of everyday life, so does the opportunity for companies to provide *educational material* for schools and colleges, and by so doing secure a place for themselves amongst an audience which within only a few years may represent a major buying potential. It is a matter of company policy whether or not to invest in the future, and this in part will be determined by the extent to which a product is amenable to brand loyalty. Even now when intensive marketing techniques and product development encourages rapid switching from one brand to another, there remain firmly entrenched products that appear capable of standing up to all forces of competition. Early impressions are important here, and where better to start than by establishing a true and fair reputation in schools whilst at the same time providing useful educational material. Leaflets, posters, charts, visual aids all have a part to play and need not be unduly expensive items. Indeed, if properly conceived a charge can be made to offset the expense of production.

With the growing importance of world trading, it is important to consider publications in an international context. If foreign language versions are likely to be of value, then the cost of production can be reduced considerably by making provision for this at the preparatory stage so that a basic format can be printed into which various languages can be slotted at minimal additional cost. It is vital that translations are thoroughly vetted so as to come across as being authentic, but this applies to a job whether it is produced as part of a well planned and econonical package or whether as an expensive afterthought.

Print or literature does not become a 'medium' until it is distributed and therefore the method of distribution needs to be thought out from the beginning. This need not be expensive even if items have to be mailed out individually, providing the mailing list is well prepared and accurate. But there are many other means of distributing literature that involve little or no cost. It can be handed out by salesmen, put on display at exhibitions, distributed at conferences, and included with other mailings. Furthermore, a valuable demand can be created by mentioning it in existing advertisements, referring to it in other publications, and by publicity in the editorial columns of the press.

## Editorial Publicity

Securing publicity in the editorial columns of the press (and in television and radio) is often regarded as the cornerstone of public relations. Whilst this is not necessarily so, the fact is that such publicity can be of considerable value in its own right, whilst in comparison with other means of communication it has special advantages. First, research has shown that editorial material is read by a higher proportion of readers than advertisements, and second, the message which appears has an implied support from the publication and is not therefore regarded as being partisan or biased.

In answer to those who like to regard editorial publicity as a cheap alternative to advertising, it should be remembered that the company concerned has no control over what appears if indeed anything is printed at all. Moreover, an item will be published only once, and even then the timing is a matter for the editorial staff alone. As regards costs, it is happily true that no payment is made to a journalist for writing an article about a company or product and whilst the preparation of material for the press involves a tangible expense, this is not usually of the same order as the cost of inserting advertisements.

Publications here can be broken down into five main groups: national newspapers, provincial newspapers, weekly newspapers, class magazines and trade and technical magazines.

These represent a major opportunity for publicity which it would be foolish to ignore. It is surprising to find the extent to which all such publications rely on material being 'sent in' to fill their editorial columns. And it is little short of incredible to discover the extent to which companies ignore these opportunities, perhaps through lack of time; sometimes through sheer ignorance.

Basically the press is interested in securing news items or features. In satisfying the need for news, publications rely heavily on *press releases* from organisations about people, products, contracts, re-equipment, innovations, achievements, exports, research work, as well as set-backs, disasters, disputes and the like. The preparation and distribution of press releases are specialist functions and no attempt will be made here to deal with this in any detail. It is worthwhile, however, paying regard to certain basic criteria which are ignored time after time. The first requirement is that a release must contain news of consequences, not to the company, but to the ultimate readers. In this respect, an outside PR consultant can be helpful in that he is likely to be more objective and to have sufficient independence to make his point known, but he is not essential and may be substituted by an internal staff member with suitable flair. A further requirement is that the news should be relevant to the readers of a particular publication and since there might be say 5,000 periodicals to be considered, this presents no small task to the supplier of news. A single press release for all types of publication is rarely adequate for the job and consequently tends to miss valuable opportunities, and in fact build up ill-will amongst journalists.

Where a particular news story is of sufficient importance, or where it is anticipated that questions are likely to be stimulated, *a press conference* is of value. It obviously stands a chance of securing greater impact since journalists will be directing their attention to the subject for half an hour or so as against maybe just a quick glance at a press release. Further, the discussions which take place both formally and behind the scenes can well result in greater coverage than would otherwise be obtained. Similarly with press visits to a factory or a supermarket or wherever else the subject is of interest.

*Feature articles* are in a different category. Ranging from 500 to perhaps 5,000 words they look at subject matter in depth, and are exclusive to one periodical. This is an area in which it is important to have a good relationship with the press. Features rarely arise out of a journalist's mind in isolation: they come about from an interchange of views with a variety of people ranging across a wide spectrum of subjects. Personal contact with journalists is vital here, and is not difficult or expensive to achieve. It may result in a good story, but only if this is judged to be so in terms of the readers' interests. It is as well to realise from the outset that the result might be a story which the originator regards as highly unfavourable, but that is the risk of seeking out this form of publicity. A point which should be made is that it is rare to find a journalist who will break a confidence and, by and large, a company can expect to get a fair hearing.

A further source of supply of feature material is in the form of the *contributed article* for which a fee is payable: also a *personal interview* presented in the form of a conversation. This latter is one of the most common forms of publicity on radio and television. In these media the greatest hurdle to overcome is that interviews are unscripted and are likely to be subject to nervous reactions on the part of the person being interviewed resulting in less than adequate replies being given. It may be encouraging to know that the interviewer is also subject to nervous tensions and is rarely as knowledgeable about the particular subject as the interviewee.

On editorial publicity for overseas markets there are many facilities available from Government agencies such as the Central Office of Information and even the overseas embassies. To achieve real impact, however, it is necessary to have a working knowledge of the media in each country, and this is a task for a specialist. The point is often made that the media in the United Kingdom are unique. What is not so often mentioned is that the same statement can be made of every country. Whilst it is true that good editorial publicity can be achieved on a small budget, it is important to realise that a modest investment in doing the job properly is likely to be most worthwhile. A good writer is every bit as necessary as for an advertisement – more so in fact, as the story will often be accepted or rejected on the basis of how well it is presented. Equally so with supporting material such as photographs and diagrams. There is no logic behind spending large sums of money on such items for advertisements and literature, only to cut back on material for the press.

*Advertising*

To some it may seem strange to include advertising in a chapter on public relations, especially so when this subject is dealt with in some detail later in the book.[1] In that instance, however, it is examined in relation to sales promotion, whereas here it is considered as a means of public relations. A common misunderstanding is to suppose that advertising and public relations are two different functions, one concerned with selling goods, the other with building up a reputation or an image. This is not so. Advertising is a channel of persuasive communications which happens to be particularly effective in many area of sales promotion. In certain circumstances it can be equally relevant in achieving public relations goals. In addition there are numerous instances of sales promotion activities not involving advertising at all, and sometimes relying largely upon editorial publicity to secure sales leads.

Consider the examples cited earlier of typical public relations objectives. There will be instances where traditional PR techniques, like editorials and special events will not easily arise, maybe because the product is fundamentally uninteresting. Raw materials often come into this category and the point is well-illustrated by reference to major press and television campaigns to promote the image and the use of steel, aluminium and leather. Another example is a company that wished to expand its selling activities into new but related products, and to do this by acquisition. It found that whilst being a major manufacturer within its industry, it was virtually unknown outside and was unlikely to be able to raise the required capital for new ventures. By a simple sample research it established its 'level of knowledge' amongst potential investors, then started on an intensive advertising campaign. It took two years before on subsequent testing it found that it had achieved sufficient recognition to be able to set about raising capital for increasing sales by acquisition, in itself a quite common marketing technique.

[1]See chapter 7 ('Advertising and Sales Promotion on a Small Budget').

Prestige advertising has earned for itself a poor reputation as being wasteful. This may have been so, but there is no longer justification for such campaigns to involve any more wastage than any form of marketing activity. After all, a sales call can turn out to be a waste. The essence of using advertising efficiently for public relations purposes is to ensure that 'before and after' research is carried out. This applies even more so than in some promotional advertising where at least there are indicators such as sales figures, retail audits, and representatives' reports. Using inexpensive postal questionnaire or even structured interview techniques a research exercise can effectively establish an initial 'benchmark' against which the impact of the campaign can be measured.[1] The advertising can then be beamed at target audiences, and the effects noted by subsequent follow-up research. This technique has been adopted very successfully in monitoring the effect of the Campaign for Company Pensions launched in 1973.

A final consideration of advertising in the public relations function is to support the publicity leading up to a major event which is itself concerned with public relations, for instance a conference or a seminar. It need hardly be said that every advertisement, as with every exposure of the company to the public eye, is automatically contributing to a company's image. This applies as equally to letterheads, vehicles, outdoor signs, salesmen's suits, company vehicles and switchboard operators as to traditional sales promotional media such as advertising, posters, point-of-sales and packaging.

*Exhibitions and Displays*

As with advertising, exhibitions are dealt with elsewhere in this book as a part of sales promotion techniques. Nevertheless, they often have an important role to play in public relations and their cost need not be excessive. True, with many large public exhibitions the impressive stands are expensive, and often rightly so, but a lavish presentation is frequently noticed more by the exhibitors concerned than by the visiting public. Agricultural shows, trade association conferences, local company sponsored events all offer important public relations opportunities which can be mounted on a relatively low budget. If the display is sufficiently interesting to visitors the expense which is put into the presentation need not be of great significance. The Farnborough Air Show is an example of the use of an exhibition for public relations purposes, where many firms set up a centre which is concerned largely with providing an opportunity for meeting customers and entertaining them without any direct relationship to the selling function.

With many public exhibitions, shell schemes are available which can

[1]See chapter 5 ('Marketing Research on a Small Budget').

be furnished with display boards which are re-usable on other occasions, and indeed, the very furnishing can be owned by the company and used for one show after another.

Just as important as mounting any kind of display on a small budget, or even a large one, is to ensure that the maximum use of the investment is made. Here many firms fall down by concentrating their energies exclusively into putting on their particular show and passively waiting for the visitors to stream in. It is much more efficient to take these as an added bonus and to set to work ensuring that all the people who are considered to be of importance are invited to come, and with some attractive reason given for their sparing the time to do so.

*Conferences and Seminars*

In almost all marketing campaigns, small specialist groups can be identified whose goodwill is particularly important. Where this is so, an inexpensive way of gaining contact and influence is by means of some kind of meeting. Face-to-face contact after all has the merit of greater impact than, say, the written word, and even though a meeting might not be in the form of a direct selling operation, there is some value in having an audience involved for a few hours in a function on a subject which is related to a product. Rarely does a company sponsor a seminar which is so attractive that an entrance fee can be charged with the result that a profit is made, or least-costs are covered.

However, there are many opportunities for organising seminars. The launch of a new range of transistors could include a seminar dealing with the technical applications of this kind of device. A plastic available in sheet form might provide an opportunity for a meeting to discuss, and have demonstrated, its application to the packaging of foodstuffs. Dealer conferences are commonplace and can reasonably fall into the public relations function. So also in consumer marketing can demonstrations and illustrated talks to certain key groups of housewives. Very small and informal luncheon parties with pressure groups, say MPs or leaders of trade associations, can be most effective in getting across an important message at an expense of no more than a few tens of pounds. Clearly, the need in all these cases is to define accurately whom it is wished to influence, then the cost reduces accordingly. In the sector of public or 'association' conferences, it is often possible to collaborate with the organisers to have a member of staff included amongst the list of speakers. The prestige is valuable in itself, but with it goes the opportunity of putting across a point of view which is conducive to the kind of business a company is conducting.

*Audio-visual*

Audio-visual techniques are fast developing and in doing so are providing new opportunities, sometimes at very low cost, for communication to both small and large audiences. The conventional sponsored film continues to represent a high investment if it is done properly, and professionalism is necessary here since viewers will tend automatically to relate the quality of presentation with what they see in cinemas and on television.

Film strips, colour slides, records, tapes and cassettes can all be produced well at a much lower cost and can be used with impact for audiences of half a dozen, or can be mailed out to large numbers of individuals or groups of people to whom both the method of presentation and perhaps the novelty will ensure a good return for the money spent. It is surprising how slow some of these inexpensive techniques are to catch on with professional communicators such as seminar leaders, educationalists, and even the clergy. Audio-visual aids have the merit of either enlivening a personal presentation, or indeed, of supplanting it.

### Planning and Co-ordination

A good number of public relations opportunities occur without any warning, and completely at random. The placing of a large contract, a new appointment, a technological discovery, a visit by a VIP, and so on. Such events often lead people to suppose that planning, therefore, has no part to play in a public relations operation. This is not so. Many activities can be forecast well in advance, for instance the launch of a new product may well take a year or more, or the building of a new factory to increase the output of an existing product may run into several years.

The need for planning is evidenced by the effect which can be achieved by the careful preparation of public relations events which are first, well-based, and second, are timed to fit in with other parts of the marketing mix. A good example is the launching of a new car where there is considerable potential interest amongst the general public, the enthusiast, the trade, and overseas markets. Often planned to coincide with a major international exhibition, there is considerable scope for building up an awareness that important news of some kind is about to break. This precedes a methodical plan embracing distribution of promotional material and products themselves to the major outlets. At the national and international level there can be a preview for the press, a function for major potential buyers, and maybe a personality to be coupled with the launch. This will normally result in feature articles and television programmes coinciding with the launching date. Over and above this are the conventional press and television advertisements, point-of-sale material, labels, stickers, salesmen's briefings and sales kits, dealer's kits and all the rest of the marketing mix.

Whilst the launching of a new car is on a large scale compared with the majority of activities in which businesses are engaged, the interlocking of promotional plans is equally valid for a specialised machine tool, a new quality of house brick, or a local taxi service. The following impact diagram shows some of the forces which can be brought to bear on a prospective customer. Other things being equal, the more times a customer is exposed to a message and the greater the variety of media which carries it, the higher will be the impact.

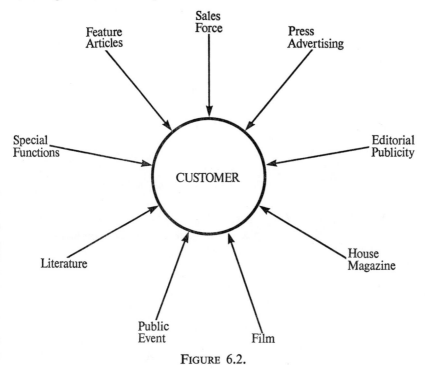

FIGURE 6.2.

*Impact Diagram*

It is not suggested that all forms of persuasive communication must be used in order to achieve results. Merely that they should all be considered, and rejected or used on the basis of their value to the campaign in relation to their cost. A new product of high intrinsic interest may provide so many opportunities in editorial publicity, in conferences and special events that no initial advertising is required. Or the market may be so specialised that the few dozen buyers can be reached by direct mail, personal calls and samples. However, a household product, which differs only marginally from those already on the market, may provide little scope for editorial publicity and here, advertising, dealer offers, merchandising and competitions are called for.

Just as important as which media to use is the need for timing. Perhaps an unconventional point of view, but nonetheless true, is the fact that news is not made when an event happens, but rather when it is announced.

Clearly, this is not true of everything, but a new application for an existing product can be held back until it is considered that an announcement will have the greatest effect. Similarly, a factory can be 'opened' any time within a year or so of its starting up. Staged events can be put on at the most opportune moment, and feature stories can usually be scheduled to within a short span of time. Obviously this can be important where seasonal factors influence purchasing for instance. But even on a longer time base, there are matters which need to be considered such as the current level of affluence, credit restrictions, trade disputes, even public opinion and fashion. Public relations for gas appliances may well change when a gas industrial dispute is in the offing, or an argument about natural gas, or the announcement of a rise in tariffs.

### Specialised Public Relations

Within any total grouping of people, whether of customers, employees, investors or local community, there will be found to exist groups which for one reason or another are of special importance. With employees, for example, the various trade union officials could be regarded as key people in getting across a point of view. With customers the same applies, for, say, the top 10 per cent, though sometimes in a more complex form.

Securing the support of the National Council of Women for a new type of consumer product might benefit a company in two ways. First, the members could be regarded as customers in themselves and second, because of their place in society, their influence upon other women could do much to help establish and publicise a new idea. Approaches to such groups which are small relative to the total market can obviously be made on a much lower budget and with perhaps greater effect than a broader appeal. If the nature of a product is such that it commends itself to certain specialised groups, then these can be regarded as the first line of approach – as key targets in the dissemination of information. Not only are they smaller, but they are homogeneous and often so structured as to make communication an easy matter. They will sometimes have their own magazine, a network of local branches with officers sitting on regional and national committees, and maybe a national conference. Examples of specialised groups are legion – women's institutes, allotment holders, fishing clubs, drama groups, the Red Cross, scouts and guides, political parties, welfare organisations, play groups, Rotary and Round Table. But even these examples fall short in that they ignore the more official groupings, for instance, the police, nurses, local government officers, teachers, doctors, the Institute of Electrical Engineers, the Scientific Instrument Manufacturers Association and so on.

No text on specialised groups can set about being comprehensive. The need here is to take the market as a whole and to segment it as in the marketing strategy, where the breakdown is to identify collective buying groups. The main purpose here is more with collective communications groups. It does in the long run amount to the same thing, that is, securing a maximum of influence at a minimum expense. The building-up of a pressure group comprising maybe only a handful or so of influential people can be a most worthwhile public relations activity. And the results of such action can far outweigh the cost and effort of doing it. Pressure groups should not be regarded as some insidious means of achieving an immoral end which if care is not exercised will bring everyone into disrepute. This is not to say that shady deals are not conducted under certain circumstances, but then that is true of human behaviour in general. Let such operations be conducted openly so that all concerned are aware of what they are being asked to do. In that way an approach can quite satisfactorily be made to precisely whomsoever one chooses. After all, they do not have to listen: indeed they may take a contrary view and set up in opposition.

A small group of people, then, can be set up to consider a proposition which a company has to make. This could be in relation to the level of tax on a product, or that the world would be a better place if everyone could be supplied with one free of charge on the National Health, or that the principal competitor should be subject to a more stringent safety regulation, or that imports should be banned, or exports subsidised. Clearly, the people chosen for a pressure group will vary widely and may include MPs, heads of trade associations, eminent educationalists, architects, police chiefs, Lord Mayors, editors of national newspapers and so on, but in every case they must be people who are genuinely sold on the cause and who are influential.

## Organising for Public Relations

Before considering the organisation, it is necessary to look to the nature of the company concerned. Whilst in this book, emphasis is laid upon the achievement of results on a small budget, it does not follow that the firm itself is small. Many firms, small both in turnover and employees, have very large marketing budgets, for instance, in fast moving consumer products. As against this there are very large companies, for instance those manufacturing and processing raw materials, which are able to operate on very small marketing budgets.

It is often said, and rightly, that in a small firm it is primarily the chief executive who directs and largely carries out the public relations function. Also true is that every employee has a public relations role to play, and this should be encouraged. In the majority of companies there will be a board of directors encompassing the principal management functions of finance, production and marketing, perhaps with the addition of research or technical, and personnel. The public relations activities usually fit in as part of the marketing operations of a company even though they may become involved in other aspects of the business. In larger firms there may be a marketing manager or publicity manager, and here the public relations officer may be on equal level or alternatively part of their staff. A different, and sometimes more satisfactory basis, is for the public relations officer to report directly to the chief executive. There is only one rule which can be laid down without fear of contradiction, and that is that unless the public relations function is positioned close to top management with every access to policy-makers and with authority to apply initiative, then it will not be effective.

There are classically three ways of organising for public relations – to handle it entirely within the company, to put in out to a PR consultancy, or to use a combination of both. There is some evidence to suggest that the latter solution is proving to be the most effective. Reasons for this are not hard to find. The company man is obviously very close to the needs of the business and also to the sources of information which are required to sustain a public relations programme. However, he suffers from company constraints and is not always in the best position to view matters objectively: neither is his advice necessarily regarded as highly as that from someone outside. A further consideration for a small-budget operation is that to do the job properly he must be a specialist, and it is therefore necessary to employ a full-time man with a secretary and with accompanying overheads.

A PR consultancy is not cheap, but can be engaged at less than the cost of setting up an in-company operation. It suffers from the lack of personal contact and detailed knowledge of the business. It has the advantage of being able to call upon the consolidated knowledge of its executives and giving impartial advice which sometimes is found to be more readily acceptable.

For the smaller firm a practical solution is often to designate the PR function to a member of staff who has some other primary responsibility. The advantage is obviously to keep expense to a minimum, and equally obvious is the fact that the job is likely to be performed less satisfactorily. In a business world where communications are becoming more and more vital, and techniques more sophisticated, the need for professional advice is growing and should only be discounted as a last resort. Evidence of professionalism is not hard to find since growing numbers of practitioners are members of the Institute of Public Relations, and consultancies are fast developing standards within the Public Relations Consultancy Association. There is now a nationally recognised qualification in public relations, namely, the CAM (Communications Advertising and Marketing) Certificate and the CAM Diploma.

**Measuring Results**

Much of the poor reputation which has laid upon the practice of public relations has been due to the difficulty of assessing results. This position is changing as techniques are developed which enable a firm to judge the effectiveness of its public relations activities. Such techniques are dealt with in the chapter on market research, but first there must be conscious effort to use this facility and with it to involve some expense. Costs of measuring results need not be prohibitive and if used properly will more than repay the investment. The essential starting point for measuring results must be in the careful definition of objectives. These should be written down, and wherever possible in quantified form. In public relations, where results are sometimes long-term, it is also important to arrange for feed-back as a continuous process rather than an investigation as and when the need arises or, more likely, after the need has passed. As with advertising and all other parts of the marketing mix, consideration should be given to each of the developing research techniques covering markets, purchasing patterns, consumer attitudes, brand awareness, media coverage, readership data, as well as conventional desk research.

### Budgeting for Public Relations

Take first the task to be performed or the objective to be reached by the public relations operation, and relate this to the overall marketing mix. From this will emerge a public relations plan which in the best judgement of the person concerned will achieve the goal. The ingredients now can be costed quite simply and the expenditure viewed from the standpoint of the value to the company of achieving the objectives: also from the point of view of the money available. 'But what will it actually cost?' is a question that no textbook can set out to answer. Examples can be given of a press release which will cost £20; a leaflet, £100; a film, £1,000: but equally, a film can be produced for £100 or £10,000 and a leaflet for £10 or £1,000. Neither can any easy formula be applied such as a percentage of sales or of advertising, or a sum based upon last year's expenditure or profit, or what a competitor is spending. Without the objectives, albeit a very practical business of the 'task', public relations cannot hope to contribute to the effective and profitable operation of a business in a meaningful way.

## CHECKLIST

- What are the company's PR objectives?

- What audience is the organisation attempting to reach?

- How large are the target audiences?

- What messages are to be transmitted and why?

- Have the messages been tailored to suit each segment of the total audience?

- Have the alternative methods of communicating with each public been evaluated?

- Have the least effective media been eliminated from the PR mix?

- Is the quality of the PR material the minimum acceptable given the objectives, the target audiences and the budget available?

- Is maximum use being made of the least-cost PR techniques?

- Are the designers of PR material concentrating on content rather than presentation?

- Have steps been taken to ensure that PR material is reaching the audiences and that wastage is minimised?

- What personnel are available for PR tasks?

# CHAPTER 7

# Advertising and Sales Promotion on a Small Budget

By John Naylor

What is a small budget in advertising terms? Often the impression gained from the advertising press is that accounts worth £100,000 or more are commonplace and anything less is hardly worth a mention. The truth is that the majority of advertisers spend a fraction of this amount and the majority of agencies are very glad to have them.

Whether an account is classed as large or small depends entirely on the person making the classification. In any case it is a meaningless exercise. What most agencies are interested in, and all should be, is whether an account, be it large or small, can be operated at a profit. And what the advertising press should be concentrating on is how to make advertising more effective; how advertisers large and small can obtain better value per pound of budget.

There is no doubt that large and small advertisers have much to learn from one another. In particular the smaller man can often demonstrate the cheaper, yet equally effective, way of doing things. His common failing, however, is to concentrate too much on cost-cutting and short-term benefits, forgetting the grand strategy and long-term plan. This usually is where the bigger man scores.

The aim of this chapter, therefore, is to try and combine the benefits of both camps. To establish how much should really be budgeted and how to derive the maximum benefit from it in both the long and the short term. It has been said that half the money spent on advertising is wasted; it is hard to disagree, and here are a few ideas which should help reduce such wastage.

### Are Advertising and Sales Promotion Necessary?

Of course, the quickest way to eliminate wasteful expenditure is to stop spending. There are still those who believe that advertising is unnecessary:

sales managers who think that their £3,000 advertising budgets would be better spent on extra salesmen, production managers who would rather spend it on machine tools. In certain cases they may be right but only if they are selling a product for which the market is extremely small and well defined. Then it becomes a simple matter of economics to determine the best way of approaching their few customers. Even here, though, some form of sales promotion should be considered. For instance, a well-known property company recently organised an extremely successful direct mail campaign to only fifty key people. (At £50 a shot!)

Advertising is not in competition with sales. The two work side by side as elements in the marketing mix. Only in mail order does advertising assume the salesman's function and usually their roles are distinct. Advertising conveys a selling message quickly to a much wider audience than a sales force could reach. Where necessary it can isolate the more likely prospects for a product hence increasing sales force efficiency. Most important of all, however, advertising gives a product added values which no salesman could ever impart.

There is a well-known remark guaranteed to provoke any salesman: 'What you will take half-an-hour to say, we have to fit into a thirty-second commercial.' This, of course, is rubbish. A commercial can only put over a single simple selling message; it is up to the salesman, packaging, point-of-sale, and other promotional aids to say the rest.

### So How Much Should Be Spent?

Different companies use different methods to calculate their advertising budgets. Some are good, some less so and some are positively bad. Perhaps the worst method, or rather lack of method, is the arbitrary figure settled in a matter of minutes and based, if anything, on previous years' expenditure levels. Apparently many companies still fix their budgets this way so that what they spend bears no direct relationship to sales past, present or future, nor to the job to be done. Research carried out two years ago revealed that many firms work to a 'fixed figure'.[1] This presumably means that their budgets remain the same year in, year out. The dangers of this approach in times of high inflation are obvious.

Equally dangerous is the budget related to competitive activity. 'They are doing it. Perhaps we should go one better.' This always presupposes that what the competition are doing is right.

More sensible budgets are those based on historical, current or forecast sales performance, or a combination of these. At least they give an indication of what the firm can afford to spend, although a budget based on historical sales has obvious limitations. Forecast sales are the most obvious criterion on which to base budget calculations, since spending is then related directly to objectives.

[1] N. A. Hart, *Industrial Publicity*, Associated Business Programmes (London, 1971).

Finally there is the task method. In theory the system is, as its name implies, a way of determining the correct budget for the job to be done. The technique used is first to define the objectives. Then to decide on the most efficient promotional way of achieving them. Costed-out this provides the optimum budget. The task method does have one major drawback, however: advertising is not a precise art. So if events do not work out quite as expected, it is possible to end up in a loss situation. Obviously, this has to be allowed for and tight controls imposed to ensure that it cannot happen.[1]

There are many other ways to set budgets but none of them is perfect. The method used by my present company is one of the most sensible. Here, the total advertising budget per country is set at a level which should enable the subsidiary concerned to achieve its key marketing and, ultimately, profit objectives. Within this total budget, however, maximum flexibility is permitted by campaign and across the whole range of products. In essence, therefore, this is the task method with an overall top limit relating to forecast sales.

In the end, there is no right or wrong way to set budgets. But to avoid money being wasted, a common-sense approach should be used. Firstly set clear marketing objectives and then fix the advertising budget. That should not be the end, however, as the budget should always be re-examined to see whether it can be reduced by 25 per cent and still achieve the same results. All budgeted items should be considered individually and pounds pared off wherever possible, particularly where unnecessary duplication of spending has crept in. It should always be remembered that it is the budget per job that counts, not the total budget.

### Is an Agency to Help Spend It?

It is quite easy for anyone with the money to recruit a good artist, copywriter, freelance media man or any other services he requires. If he has the time and if he knows where to go, that is. It is also possible for any company to establish its own advertising department and dispense with the need for an agency completely.

Whether any small to medium advertiser really benefits from using an agency is still a matter for debate. Much depends on the particular circumstances. For most companies the main advantage of using an agency is that the majority of services required are housed under one roof and usually they are all of a reasonable standard. When working under pressure it is very convenient to be able to pick up the telephone, or call them round, brief them on requirements and then forget about the problem until they come back with their proposals. It is possible to be rid of many problems and masses of detail work in this way.

[1]Alexander, Cross and Hill, *Industrial Marketing*, Richard D. Irwin (Homewood, Ill., 1967), pp. 420–422.

Almost certainly the agencies do not see themselves in this light. An agency asked to justify its role will probably argue that they can offer unbiased objective opinions on their client's plans and ideas, or that the client will benefit from their wide experience of his own and related markets. In the case of the large grocery suppliers, both of these arguments could possibly be valid, but they are in the realms of fantasy as far as smaller advertisers are concerned. Staff working on small accounts are under pressure from a number of clients. It is most likely that they will know much less about each company's market than the company itself does and will be only too delighted to accept the client's ideas if they seem reasonable.

As always the clients of advertising agencies get what they pay for. A small budget advertiser can expect the following for his money:

● The use of experienced advertising personnel.

● Efficient service, i.e. what he wants produced on time.

● Sensible advice on advertising and marketing techniques.

● A reasonable standard of creative work.

● A detailed knowledge of advertising media with good media buying facilities.

● Possibly a merchandising and packaging unit.

● Possibly a market research department or facility.

● Probably no knowledge whatever of his product, his market or his particular problems. But most are willing to learn and advise.

It might be thought that this sounds like an argument for employing more staff on the company payroll or building up an advertising department. So it could be. The major objections to this are cost, recruiting the people of the calibre of agency people and keeping them fully employed.

How much should agency services cost? Sometimes nothing, sometimes very little. It all depends on the distribution of expenditure and, or course, the value of the total advertising budget. The present commission system dates back to the time when agencies were representatives of the media, offering their services free to advertisers. The publishers then paid them commission based on a fixed percentage of the cost of the space booked. Even though they are no longer linked to the media, they still receive this commission, which pays in part for their services to their clients, assuming, that is, they want to use media advertising.

The current trend is towards a guaranteed minimum income system whereby the client agrees to pay the agency a fixed sum monthly based on estimated expenditure and the likely work involved. The agency then credits the client with all commissions received and bills the difference. This seems fair and sensible and also overcomes the main objection to the old commission system: namely that it helps to discourage agencies from recommending media advertising where other forms of promotion would be more logical.

The golden rule when agreeing a fee with an agency is not to agree too readily. Unless your spending is likely to be confined to media advertising alone, there is no sure way of fixing the amount precisely. The budget-conscious client is advised to try and bargain to a figure a little below what he is finally prepared to pay – with the offer of a review at the end of the first six months or year. What have you got to lose?

## Choosing an Agency

Most agencies claim to be all things to all men! Few are. They all have their strengths and weaknesses and that is why accounts keep moving around. Which agency is exactly right for any given company is seldom likely to be discovered. A planned and systematic approach in selecting an agency, however, can eliminate many of the uncertainties. There are many differences in the service which can be obtained for scarce pounds. There are over eight hundred advertising agencies in the United Kingdom plus dozens of smaller creative units, creative consultants, 'hot-shops', call them what you will, so that some kind of screening is essential.

To do this it is first essential to know what is wanted by defining requirements as specifically as possible. Start with the product. Who buys it? How is it sold? Would an agency require specialised knowledge to write about it? Would it be advertised in national, local, trade or technical press? Does it need packaging or point-of-sale support? How big is the budget? These are pointers towards the type of agency required. Answers may not be available to all of these questions but it is as well to sort out as many as possible.

What next? Well, there is no cut-and-dried procedure. The best results usually come from testimonials.

Examining the work carried out for another company in a related field, seeking opinions from trade associations, discussing the problem with the free advisory service of the Institute of Practitioners in Advertising may all help to narrow the field. As many agencies as possible should be given a preliminary examination; it costs nothing other than time and what are a few days amortised over the years that the agency might be employed? Arising out of this examination of alternatives a short-list should be drawn up of the three or four agencies which are considered best suited to requirements. Each of these should be invited to your premises to give a brief presentation to you and your colleagues. Do not ask them to produce speculative layouts: they cannot possibly know enough about your products to do a sensible job at this stage. Just sit back and judge them as people. As a team. Examine the work they have done for other clients over the past few months. Find out how long the team has been together and whether they are likely to remain so. (Advertising people have a nasty habit of moving on just after you have appointed them.) What is the total range of services that they offer? And so on. Give them a hard time for an hour or two then let them go.

Do exactly the same with each agency and carefully note the strengths and weaknesses of each. Your colleagues should do the same. When you compare notes, you will be surprised how one agency stands head and shoulders above the rest – for your needs, that is.

**Added Values**

What can be done to stretch an inadequate budget even further? Can advertising do more for a client than it is doing at present? Frequently advertising is used solely to convey a selling message to the maximum number of people or to produce sales leads; or to help sell into stockists. Consumer research has in recent years shown up an effect of advertising that has been neglected by all but a few of the more enlightened advertisers: the establishment of a brand identity. There is no doubt that advertising can contribute intangible added values to any product.

In tests on household and grocery products it has been shown that, when faced with a choice of two similar unnamed products, roughly equal numbers of people choose each one. When, however, the two products are named, significant differences in choice occur. These differences can only be attributed to brand preferences created through advertising.

Going one stage further, a group of housewives were questioned on the personalities of various branded products. They were asked to imagine products as people and describe what sort of personalities they would have. The results were amazing and remarkably consistent. Persil, for instance, was considered by some as happy and contented and by others as dull and lacking in ambition. The same thing seen from different points of view.

If you are not involved in fast moving consumer goods you must be thinking 'Well, how does this affect me?' It does. Consider the hypothetical case of an electronic equipment manufacturer faced with the choice of buying his components from a well-known manufacturer such as Motorola or from a small local manufacturer offering similar components of equal quality, but which are unknown in the market place. He may be happy with the local man's products but what will his customers think? Will they be happy to buy an expensive piece of equipment containing components bearing an unknown name?

What advertising can do for any firm and its products is to create an image. An authority. A brand or corporate personality. Public confidence. This is an added benefit of advertising and sales promotion when planned.

It can work against you if it remains unconsidered. The next step, therefore, is to define your creative strategy.

## Creative Strategy

Persil must surely be one of the most successful brands on the market today. It has held its share of the total washing powder market for a long time, in spite of assaults from many brands of detergent and biological powder. The principal lessons that can be learnt from Persil are twofold: the importance of accurate market positioning and continuity of advertising theme. Right from the start the company established to whom they were talking and the message they wanted to convey. Their creative strategy has remained virtually unchanged to the present day.

The most important first step in advertising therefore is to decide, precisely, the target audience to be reached in as much detail as possible: age, sex, social grades, special interests. It is surprising how many people, including some agency personnel, skate over the surface of this vital subject. In selling to industry in particular one must endeavour to cover everyone of influence in the purchasing decision and the buying chain can be quite long.

Having decided on the audience the next step is to consider the message. On advertising agency (J. Walter Thompson) has attempted to formalise this procedure with their 'T-Plan,' the platform on which all creative strategy is based. Other agencies adopt similar methods.

FIGURE 7.1.

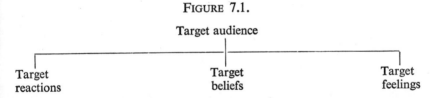

Basically the idea is that advertisers are not really interested in what goes into their material but what comes out: what people immediately notice in the brand (target reactions), what they should believe about the brand (target beliefs), and what they should feel towards the brand (target feelings) as a result of product design, creative and media strategies.

Taking our hypothetical electronic equipment manufacturer as an example, a T-Plan for his latest electronic voltmeter might look something like this:

Target audience: Purchasing officers, design and test engineers, senior management in the electrical and electronic component manufacturing industries; purchasing officers, electronic design and test engineers in the aircraft industry; purchasing officers, design and test engineers in the computer industry.

Target reactions: That looks a smart piece of equipment. Clear readout. I have not seen one like that before.

Target beliefs: It is a well made instrument. It will do everything we need it for and more besides. It is so simple even an idiot apprentice could use it safely.

Target feelings: We ought to have one if we are to keep up to date.

Obviously these targets are fictitious but should convey the general principle. The most important thing to remember is that, having established a creative strategy, it is used as the basis for all material relating to that product: including advertising, packaging and point-of-sale. Where possible it should also have an influence on the design of the product itself.

Millions of pounds a year are wasted on advertising that is badly briefed, ill-conceived and often produced on an *ad hoc* basis with no continuity of creative approach. The cost is more than it appears. What these advertisers are throwing away are the opportunities to create strong brand identities for their products. You would not find Procter & Gamble or Unilever doing this, nor Sony or Hoover. All of these household names have worked hard to establish the brand names they own. So must every advertiser, large or small.

## Setting Objectives

In attempting to justify advertising expenditure, it is often said that one cannot attribute any success wholly to the effects of advertising as so many other factors are involved, in particular, selling effort. It's funny that one never hears the reverse argument. Nor does one ever hear of an advertising man being given commission on sales. Salesmen as a matter of course tend to hog the successes. As the old saying goes: 'When sales are going well, it's good selling. When sales are going badly, it's bad advertising.'

The advertising business itself is largely to blame for this state of affairs. For years it has operated in a hit and miss fashion. Millions of pounds have been frittered away on campaigns with no set objectives. In many cases the only reason for advertising has been that it was considered the thing to do when, for example, one launched a new product. 'Showing the flag' is hardly a justification for spending thousands.

The growth of interest in marketing has tended to improve this situation. Marketing plans are now being written in various shapes and forms and most include a section on advertising and sales promotional activity. But set advertising objectives are still a rarity.

For obvious reasons, most advertising objectives are defined merely in qualitative terms. Wherever possible, however, quantifiable targets should be produced. Ideally, for instance, the effectiveness of mass media advertising should be measured by market research. If, for one reason or another, this is impossible, then at least an attempt should be made to quantify the coverage of the target audience that has been achieved.

Results from direct mail activity are much easier to assess. Here one should be looking for percentage response, conversion into orders and cost-effectiveness measured in terms of cost per enquiry or sale. Remember, though, that direct mail is not always intended to produce replies. It is often used simply to inform or influence opinion. Even when used to pull enquiries it has some effect on many of the people who have not replied.

### The Right Media

Media selection is as much a part of the creative process as designing the advertisement. Or it should be. The first requirement of any advertisement is to attract attention. Yet the strange thing is that whilst a visualiser might spend days devising ways and means of gaining attention, the amount of time spent on deciding the size of space and media to be used is a minute fraction of this.

The most common failing is to go for the obvious solutions without considering the full range of possibilities. The right starting point is the target audience. How many ways are there of reaching these people? Which are the most cost-effective ways? Which are ways best suited to our product? Does it benefit from being demonstrated, for example? Would colour help? What would make our advertisement stand out from its rivals?

No solution should ever be accepted without covering every other possibility. Just because no-one else has done it before does not mean to say that it is wrong. On the contrary, that could be the very reason why it should be tried.

### Television on a Small Budget

Television is a very under-rated medium, by the small-budget advertiser, that is. For some reason, many companies never consider it because, it seems, they tend to regard it as the pressure of the big spender. They could not be more wrong. Television used nationally can be expensive but on a regional basis it can often be the most economical, and effective, solution to the advertiser's problem.

In December 1972 a print of the current Dymo commercial was sent to the company distributor in Jersey. After it had appeared three times on Channel Television he had sold his complete stock. The cost of the three spots was £21.00. This illustrates clearly the two points made above: the tremendous effectiveness of television advertising and the fact that it need not be expensive.

Television-time costs relate to the size of the viewing audience. Hence Channel Television offers the lowest rate at a basic £11[1] for 30 seconds in peak time, £4 in early evening off-peak. At the other end of the scale we have the London Region with Thames TV offering a basic peak time rate of £1,760 for a 30-second spot and £95 for 30 seconds in mid-afternoon. The total potential ITV audience in London, however, is 12·4 million adults.

Few advertisers pay the basic rate. Discount structures and special arrangements vary from region to region. But all regions have one thing in common: they are anxious to attract new advertisers. To this end, with the exception of the very cheap stations, they all offer incentives to newcomers. Usually this takes the form of a straight discount, often 30 per cent. If you can genuinely claim to be a local advertiser, not trading nationally, then you stand a chance of getting a 50 per cent discount in some areas. Television offers many bargains such as this. It is well worth reading the rate cards carefully.

Whether or not television is the right medium for your product depends entirely upon your target audience and objectives. One word of caution: the response from television is usually fast and often overwhelming. It is most important to consider whether your distributive outlets, sales force and/or switchboard are equipped to handle this demand. If half the people who respond to your advertisement cannot find your product the next day then your money is being poured down the drain. Paradoxically, television can help you to overcome this problem if you are selling through retail outlets. Shopkeepers are sold on the medium. The mere promise of television advertising makes it much easier to open new outlets.

The one aspect not mentioned yet is the commercial itself. How much will this cost? As much or as little as you want to spend is generally the answer. With one slight reservation; if you intend to shoot on location in the Bahamas, then you are in for more than a few pounds. Commercials on this sort of scale can easily cost as much as £20,000 for 30 seconds. It is also possible to produce an adequate 30-second studio commercial on video tape, for as little as £250. Normally, however, production costs start out at £3 — £4,000 for a 30-second commercial on film, £500 on videotape.

The differences between film and videotape commercials are legion, but the agencies generally prefer to use film for six main reasons:

● They retain greater control on the studio floor.

● Film is suitable for location work.

● More sensitive lighting effects are possible with film.

[1]All prices quoted were those prevailing in 1973/4.

- Film is easier to handle and distribute.

- Videotape wears out quickly.

- Advertisers usually want to show their commercials on their own premises or at sales meetings. Film is much more convenient for this purpose.

On the other hand, most television programmes are recorded on video-tape and they are of an acceptable quality. Editing is much easier as the equipment provides instant replays. And it is much, much cheaper. As a rule of thumb, therefore, it is reasonable to suggest that for simple studio commercials, without a complex set, where the message is the thing and a film festival award is not required, use videotape. You can spend the saving on more air time.

### National Press

To run a worthwhile *national* campaign on television would cost £70,000 at least: big money for a big audience covering 92 per cent of all homes. Few small budget advertisers are ready for, or even interested in, campaigns on this scale. Most products are designed to appeal only to certain sections of the population: nothing like 92 per cent. Here is where the national press comes into its own.

The press offers by far the cheapest means of reaching a national audi-ence. It can do this because its coverage is less extensive than television or, to put it more fairly, its coverage is more selective. This is its greatest virtue.

Whatever your age, sex, social status, political inclinations or special interests, there is almost certainly a national newspaper or magazine to suit you. And likewise as an advertiser you are likely to find at least one publication to match your target audience with a reasonable degree of accuracy.

In quantitative terms, it is possible, indeed usual, to plan a schedule of the most suitable publications based on data available in the National Readership Survey. Most agencies have access to this information. For the purpose of comparisons it is also usual to take the cost per thousand readers for a given publication. Ideally, however, one should attempt to estimate the cost per hundred worthwhile readers, i.e. readers within one's target audience.

Figures should not be one's only consideration however. Very often the amount of information to be conveyed determines the minimum size of space that can possibly be used. It is sometimes preferable, therefore, to take a larger space with a lesser coverage than a small space with greater coverage. The need for colour is another critical factor from both econo-mic and technical points of view. Finally, there is that mystical factor, 'atmosphere'. Some products just are not suited to certain newspapers – in spite of their coverage.

One major advantage of press over television is its ability to convey a more detailed and complex message. This can also be its undoing. Many advertisements are crammed with far too much information, generally in a stereotyped layout.

Maybe the big advertisers can afford this risk; the small budget advertiser cannot. Attention, interest, desire, action: this sequence should be ingrained in the hearts of all advertising men. Forget the attention factor and you can forget the rest too. Whereas the big advertiser by repeating his message *ad infinitum* can bank on his message getting across eventually, the small man must gain attention first time. There is no sure way of achieving this but certainly an advertisement which is bold, imaginative and *different* stands a better chance than most. Never mind the purists. You are not out for a design award. What you want is an advertisement which is noticed – and read.

Bargains are just as common in the press as they are in television. Many newspapers are on hard times and they need your business, so it is worth haggling with them. You may not get reduced rates but special positions are quite a common, and useful, bonus. One agency goes in for odd-shaped small ads for one of its clients; something like two inches across five columns. This is a perfect pest for the newspapers' make-up men as it rarely fits together with other small ads and virtually obliges them to place it amongst or alongside editorial.

Good value for money may be derived from competition sponsorship. Women's magazines in particular are always after sponsors. The basic idea is that you provide the prizes, they publicise and run the competition. If your products are suitable for use as prizes then you include those. It is a good way of getting your name over reasonably cheaply, and it is particularly useful if they have to describe what your product is and does as part of their write-up.

**Trade and Technical Press**

Of necessity, trade and technical publications are the media most used by the smaller advertiser and unfortunately they are the least satisfactory. Over 2,000 of them are listed in the current issue of British Rate and Data (BRAD).[1]

As a general rule, avoid all publications whose circulations are not audited. Just glancing through BRAD quickly you will see the words 'Figures in accordance with BRAD's requirements not received' time and

---

[1] *British Rate and Data*, published by Maclean-Hunter, is the standard reference work for anyone concerned with media selection. Published monthly on annual subscription only, it gives basic details and advertisement space/time costs for all United Kingdom advertising media: newspapers, magazines, television, posters, cinema, etc.

time again. Secondly, always insist on seeing a Media Data Form for any publication you are considering. This form is far from perfect, but at least it gives some idea of the readership of a journal as opposed to its circulation.

All one can do is to treat the information available with due scepticism. Why not conduct readership surveys amongst your own customers? This can be extremely enlightening. Read through the publications yourself. If they look like rubbish to you, other people may think so too. If you are new in a market, find out where your competitors and manufacturers of related products advertise. They may be wrong too but it is useful back-up information.

When you have finally decided on a schedule, save yourself some money and forget the covers and other special positions. There is no evidence to support the claims that they are more effective than any other position. On the contrary, researches published by McGraw-Hill and Morgan-Grampian prove that they have little extra value, if any.

In terms of advertisement content, research shows that clearly-stated technical fact is what the readers of trade and technical publications want. Cut out the gimmicks and the girls: they can often work against you in such media. Reading and noting studies conducted amongst the readers of an electronics journal a few years ago illustrated these points plainly. The most successful advertisement in the issues surveyed scored 44 per cent recall against an average of 20 per cent. Several received a zero rating. The advertisements studied included one on an inside front cover, several in facing matter positions, one or two which were in the wrong journal anyway, and they were all trying to be too clever. The winning advertisement was in a thick wedge of ads at the front of one issue and it consisted of a clear and simple statement of technical fact.

Frequency of advertising is absolutely essential. As mentioned above, the average recall rating for any advertisement was about 20 per cent. This figure is common throughout most technical publications. It usually takes a series of five or six appearances of the same advertisement to achieve anything like a 100 per cent recall. If money is tight it is better to use six half pages than three full pages. Increased size and extra colours both tend to increase the ratings but not in proportion to the added cost. The bleed[1] charge is the only expenditure over and above the standard page cost which can really be recommended. This extra expenditure more than pays for itself in added impact.

### Posters, Bus Sides, Underground Cards and Other Outdoor Media

Large-scale poster advertising is not for the small-budget advertiser. Sites

---

[1]'Bleed' is a term used to describe an advertisement in which the printed area extends to the extreme edges of the page and into the gutter, i.e. it has no white border around it.

are comparatively expensive, production costs are high and it really does not do the job that most small advertisers require. In fact, posters are generally used as a back-up to large-scale television or press advertising. They increase frequency of opportunities to see a message and tend to mop up the light ITV viewers. Their main limitation, of course, is that they can only convey a single simple message. Posters used locally, however, can occasionally be very effective. For instance, a poster sited outside the main gate of your potential customer is a good way of making sure your product is noticed and remembered by the people you want to reach in that company. Organising that particular siting, though, is likely to cause problems.

Likewise transportation advertising used as a tactical weapon can prove extremely effective at a reasonable cost. A few years ago, *Die Welt* wanted to attract more advertising from the City of London. They discovered that a certain bus route passed the offices of the majority of people whom they were trying to influence. Their bus-side posters 'Gotterdammgoodreadership' did the trick. That simple message won them the extra business at what must have been an incredibly low cost.

Advertisements in the London Underground, both in the station and 'Tube cards' in the trains, are a good way of catching the commuter traffic and Saturday shoppers. Several firms have devoted their total budgets to this form of advertising with great success. It has one advantage over posters generally in that, as the audience is virtually captive for quite long periods of time, a longer and more complex message can be conveyed. A number of advertisers such as Cockburn's Port and Dyno-Rod ('Satisfaction guaranteed, or your blockage back!') have achieved quite a following of enthusiastic readers over the years. One word of caution however: production costs are usually very high for Tube cards as they have to be supplied mounted on strawboard.

Outdoor advertising takes many forms. You will find a list of most of them at the back of British Rate and Data. You can take space in bus shelters, on public information panels, in buses, trains, taxis, ships – the list is lengthy. You can also book regular showings on newcasters[1] in London and Bristol. In every case the same arguments apply: if you have a specific local need, by all means use these media, but as a general rule they cannot and should not form the basis for any low budget national advertising campaign.

**Direct Mail**

If you can identify your audience with a reasonable degree of accuracy

---

[1]Illuminated panels on which news messages and advertisements are displayed by means of hundreds of lights switching on and off, hence giving the impression that the message is moving from right to left.

and this audience is not too extensive, use direct mail. It is several times more expensive per thousand people reached than advertising but still more economical in the many cases where the wastage factor in the circulation of a particular journal is high. And, of course, your direct mail is more likely to be read anyway.

Whether or not your mailing piece is automatically discarded by the recipient depends entirely on what it is and says. Everyone nowadays receives masses of unsolicited mail but even this has a chance to succeed. Most people glance at everything before throwing it away.

Like any other form of promotion, direct mail should begin with written objectives. And the most important of these should state whether the mailing is intended solely to produce sales leads or whether it is intended merely to inform. Most mailings fall between these two stools and this way the senders think they have failed. If you tell all in your mailpiece, the recipient makes his decision on the spot and if the decision is negative you hear no more.

A mailing, however clever, cannot reason or counter objections so it is usually wise to leave this to your salesmen. Dymo relies heavily on direct mail for selling to the commercial and industrial markets. The main objective always is to create the maximum number of good leads for the salesmen to follow up. From experience it has been found that there are two simple techniques for increasing the return from any mailing. One is to give the absolute minimum of information; just sufficient to whet the reader's appetite. Full information is offered as an incentive to reply. This works particularly well for new products, or new ideas where a 'personal preview' or something similar is offered. The other method is to offer something free. This is always a winner. As an example Dymo regularly obtains a 15–20 per cent response to mailings offering a free desk marker and consistently one in three replies is converted into an order worth an average £25. Normal returns to industrial mailings are usually between 2–5 per cent.

Just as it is extremely important to select advertising media with real care, so it is equally necessary to pick and vet the right mailing list. Ideally, of course, you should have your own and every company should aim at building up a list. Names and addresses are worth money and should be treated with the same respect. Very often, however, you will be obliged to use a mailing house. There are many of them and most can offer a wide range of lists, from bee-keepers to atomic scientists. All one can say here is: be extremely careful. Check their lists. Ask for their source and date of compilation. Go to their premises and see how they operate. Many an unwary advertising manager has spent a fortune on creativity and print only to pour it immediately down the drain by not discovering that the list he was using was ten years out of date.

**Exhibitions**

Exhibitions are expensive. They can also prove to be the most wasteful of all promotional methods, particularly the big national and international shows in London and overseas. Whether or not a company should participate in an exhibition at all depends entirely on individual circumstances. Looked at logically, the only valid reason for using any medium is that it offers greater cost-effectiveness in reaching one's target audience than other media. But how many of us are totally logical?

Seven or eight years ago, a pretty accurate way of calculating exhibition budgets was to allow £5 per square foot. £6 or £7 per square foot is nearer the mark nowadays. It is a good rule of thumb anyway for calculating the total cost of space, shell scheme, design and standfitting. Like any other form of buying, you should keep your costs down by putting the job out to quote and keeping the design simple. If the quotes seem high ask your designer to look at ways of reducing the cost. Very often you can save money simply by using different material or making a rounded corner square.

But having a beautiful stand at a reasonable price is not enough. You have to make it work. Attract people onto your stand by sending out as many invitations as you can, or by offering inducements of one sort or another, or by appointing members of your staff to stop passers-by and invite them aboard. Do not give away masses of expensive literature but produce a cheap give-away that can be handed out to everyone attending the show. All of this may sound obvious, but it is fair to say that the majority of stands at industrial and trade exhibitions are staffed by salesmen who are inadequately briefed, who stand around smoking and talking to their pals and seem frightened to talk to people unless they are asked a question.

Large-scale exhibitions suffer from the disadvantage that visitors are bombarded with too much information in too short a time. Hence the growth of local shows. The only comments one can make about these is that they must be even better planned than a stand at a big show. Given adequate preparation, however, they often do more for a company than a stand at a big show could ever do.[1]

**Point-of-Sale**

There is little doubt that it is point-of-sale material and packaging that really sell Dymo products through retail outlets rather than the limited advertising we do. Of course the two complement one another and some of the advertising, particularly that on television, creates a natural demand.

[1]For further reference see Alfred Alles, *Exhibitions: Universal Marketing Tools*, Associated Business Programmes (London, 1973).

But steady all-year-round sales are achieved by display at the point-of-sale.

Merchandising and display techniques are in a continuous state of flux. For instance, showcards which looked modern and attractive only two or three years ago now look old-fashioned and rather dull. Suppliers have to keep abreast of new developments, and the only way of doing this is to get out into the field as much as possible and see what others are doing. The cosmetics industry is worth following. Many ideas originate there. Reading the packaging, display and retail press is another method of keeping up to date.

It is also true, however, that the biggest single area of wastage in advertising today is in point-of-sale display material. To illustrate this point you have only to look in the back yard of any grocer, chemist or hardware shop.

There is little point in dwelling on design requirements as these vary according to product. Suffice it to say that, before producing anything, it is as well to conduct a small research exercise to discover whether the item you are working on will fit the location for which it is intended. This may seem obvious, but a vast number of showcards and dispensers are still being produced which only survive until the door closes behind the salesman who placed them. The biggest saving of all can be made by rationing the material issued to your sales force. Make them account for the items they place. Salesmen's garages all round Britain are overflowing with unused, and often obsolete, material.

**Packaging**

Packaging can play a marketing role equal in importance to point-of-sale material. Always bear in mind, however, that the original function of packaging was to protect the product and it still serves this purpose. Whatever the construction you decide upon, the finished job must stand up to the type of handling it is likely to receive before it reaches the ultimate consumer. You only have to watch parcels being thrown around at any railway station to see the sort of treatment your packaging must withstand. Large sums of money are wasted year in year out because this factor has been overlooked.

Then there is the question of cost. In the end, the most satisfactory pack is the one that achieves the best balance between its two roles of protective device and silent salesman – at the most economic price. Once you have found a design which seems reasonable, take a fresh look at it and ask yourself these few questions:

● Does it look bright, modern and in keeping with its target audience?

● Does it attract the eye?

● Does it promote your brand name clearly?

● Does it provide all the necessary information?

● Does it enhance the apparent value of the product?

● Will it withstand the sort of treatment it is likely to encounter?

● Could it be made more cheaply without losing the total effect by reducing the number of colours, changing the material used or simplifying the construction? Savings are nearly always possible and money saved here can have a considerable effect on your profit margin.

## Literature

Most firms spend far too much money in this area. It is the easiest thing in the world for a salesman to leave a brochure rather than take an order. So the first recommendation, therefore, is once again to ration supplies.

Generally speaking, literature can be divided into four broad categories: sales promotional material, technical specifications, instruction books, price lists. Where many people go wrong is in trying to combine two or more of these. Thus we see technical specification leaflets, often in full colour, with hard-selling copy. This is not wrong, it is wasteful. Specifications and instruction books should be simply written, easy to follow and neat. There is no need for colours except perhaps to clarify a point. Price lists too should merely be informative. They are not there to do a selling job. This is the role of sales promotional brochures and leaflets which should concentrate on the main selling features of your product using every possible technique to convert the reader. If price is a selling feature, then by all means include it. If the equipment is simple to operate, then by all means demonstrate it. But under no circumstances let your brochure or leaflet degenerate into being half promotional, half specification or the chances are that you will succeed in neither area. At the very best it will do the job, but at double the cost.

Quality in literature, as in all promotional material, is important. If it bears the name of your company then it should be good. But quality is not synonymous with colour. A black-and-white publication can look just as smart as one in four colours. Sometimes better.

## Co-operative Promotions

Anyone who sells through retail outlets must have received letters from their stockists asking for advertising in local newspaper features on the opening of their new premises or some similar event. Pure blackmail. If, however, one is obliged to go along with it for one reason or another, then an effort should at least be made to make it pay. One thing is certain; a one-off congratulatory in a local newspaper will do nothing for anyone, least of all the retailer. Every advertisement should sell your products hard. Why not produce a standard advertisement featuring a 'new premises' offer lasting one week or one month; this at least stands a chance. If the stockist can blackmail you into taking space, do not forget to turn the tables on him by asking him to take more stock to cater for likely demand!

Some co-operative promotions can be mutually profitable to you and the stockist. But, like everything else, careful planning is needed – planned advertising (costs shared?) planned point-of-sale (window and in-store displays?), planned stock levels, special offers. Looked at in this light, problems become opportunities – as the sales people are always telling us.

### Conclusion

If an advertising budget is calculated on a sensible basis, then the most important consideration is not how much it is but how the maximum benefit can be derived from it.

As in all other aspects of marketing, the road to success is through planning: assemble all known facts, write a plan with objectives; decide on the most economical promotional mix that will enable you to adhere to these objectives; execute the plan carefully and then evaluate the results. Choose the right agency. Establish a creative strategy. Consider *every* possibility and the chances are you will come out winning.

## CHECKLIST

● What was the advertising and promotion budget last year and how was this spent?

● What is the specific role to be played by advertising?

● Is advertising necessary or will other, lower cost promotional techniques be equally effective?

● What are the specific objectives of the advertising campaign?

● What message is to be conveyed?

● Who are the target audiences for advertising and can these be clearly segmented?

● Which media are most effective in reaching the target audiences?

● Is any special experience or knowledge required to advertise and promote the company's products or services?

● Which advertising agencies possess the skills and resources required and have comparable experience in comparable situations?

146 Marketing on a Small Budget

● How much of the advertising and promotional function can be carried out by your own staff?

● Has the advertising agency been correctly briefed, particularly on the budget available?

● Can the use of each of the promotional techniques be justified by its contribution to profits?

CHAPTER 8

# Sales Development on a Small Budget

BY GORDON BRAND

## Selling in the Promotional Mix

'Why do we have a sales force?' is a less than serious question asked
frequently enough when managers are confronted with long order books
and poor delivery performance or alternatively, in more depressed times,
with a warehouse bulging with apparently immovable stock. If anyone
were to take the question as non-rhetorical the answer would probably
be, 'Because we've always had one'.

Nevertheless, questions relating to the role and costs of selling are highly
relevant in terms of a total promotional budget covering advertising and
public relations as well as direct personal promotion by the sales representative. The decision as to the proportionate expenditure on selling and
advertising still has to be taken.

Marketing, with all its developments during the past twenty years, has
not, as yet, reached a point of avoiding susceptibility to fads and one
argument which goes in cycles throughout the years is that of the relative
merits of the two major forms of promotion. The high cost of the personal
approach is set against the relatively low cost per thousand customers
reached by advertising. The force of repetition offered by advertising is
compared with the inefficiency of the salesman who can only manage
some one-and-a-half hours of face-to-face sales contact in a normal
eight-hour day, the remaining time taken up with travelling, parking,
report writing, introductions and the inevitable waiting.

Taken in isolation these points of criticism and praise have some value,
but they represent the fine tuning of management which can produce
savings through the accurate selection of media or economic journey
patterns on a large territory; but such savings are small in terms of the
waste in the mis-direction of the overall promotional effort.

Real savings can be achieved by cutting through the Gordian knot of
claims and counter-claims by answering two fundamental questions:

| What is the objective? | (What is to be achieved through promotion?) |
| What is the method? | (How can the objective be reached?) |

Different companies at different times in their development will have varying objectives, but the methods used to meet those objectives are governed by the fundamental characteristics of advertising and selling.

The role of advertising is to bring the consumer from a state of unawareness through to an awareness of the product or service being offered. Persuasion can be attempted, but the creative skills of the advertising specialist are better put to the task of obtaining and maintaining the regular attention of potential customers. It is in this role that advertising is most effective; and indeed this is the basis for its social and economic justification in Western society in that for a competitive system to exist, all buyers must be aware of offers made by all sellers.

The strengths of advertising are to be found, therefore, in the widespread attention and the raising of interest through mass media. It has its limitations, however. The message cast to a wide population must be a general one saying all things to all people. Detail is restricted and the formalities for booking time or space are sufficiently strict to lead to a lack of flexibility. It is also a one-way medium. Consumers generally do not talk back to advertisements, or, at least, if they do, they cannot be heard by the people who matter.

In a contrasting, but complementary role, personal selling effort must be aimed only at a concentrated market. Selling provides a two-way channel of communication through which the prospective buyer emits buying signals which can be picked up by the salesman to guide his approach and presentation. The keynote characteristics are flexibility and adaptability. These enable the salesman to move from getting general attention and awareness to the more specific and individual task of conviction and, eventually, some definite action.

Both forms of promotion are normally associated with high cost and yet both are accepted as effective tools of marketing management. The waste occurs, as with many an endeavour, in the inappropriate use of techniques.

For example, a salesman employed simply to announce product features or benefits without the ability to listen and adapt to the reaction he receives, is carrying out a function which could be more cheaply effected by advertising. Equally, if he can raise interest and yet be incapable of closing the sale, he is performing a function more economically achieved by other means.

Direct mail can be seen as an attempt to combine the lower cost (per unit reached) of advertising with the advantages of directness and concentration of personal selling. Like most attempts to obtain the best of both worlds, something less than the idea result is normally to be accepted.

## Selling and the Marketing Concept

The widespread adoption of the marketing concept, with its emphasis on a mixture of activities, has reduced the breadth of responsibility previously accorded to sales management. With the tasks of new-product planning, marketing research and distribution taken onto other shoulders, the sales force is left free to do what it is supposed to do, that is, sell. This sharper, more defined role fits very well into the marketing concept and in no way reduces the importance of the salesman. In fact, he is given a more difficult job.

If we can accept that by marketing we mean 'serving chosen customer segments profitably', then orders picked up anywhere by a poorly directed sales force are not only unwelcome but are to be positively discouraged. The ability to harness a company's resources to the needs of customers identified as sufficiently profitable is one of the key contributions of marketing management and the responsibility for bringing this about is largely left to the sales force. It takes skill to refuse business from uneconomic customers or to explain why an unprofitable product line has been dropped without impairing the supplying company's image. It also takes ability and a highly professional brand of executive selling to put the case for more business before high level decision-makers in companies with key customer potential.

The sales force, therefore, retains its importance, albeit within more restricted terms of reference, in those companies which have accepted the implications of the marketing concept. It has also retained its traditional key role in the production-oriented company for whom it is the sole source of market contact.

The majority of businesses will accept, therefore, the essential role of the sales force. The problem is, how can a sales force be made more efficient? How can costs, relative to the value of orders gained, be reduced?

## Planning the Sales Operation

In comparison with other employees, the sales representative working a territory away from head office leads a very lonely life. If he feels a grudge against the management he cannot go along the corridor and have a self-pity session with a colleague. The only people he sees regularly are customers to whom he has to represent a well-ordered, smoothly-running organisation. Unfortunately, he is all too aware of his own company's deficiencies but he cannot afford the luxury of joining with his customer in wallowing in a criticism of those deficiencies. He has to play it straight knowing that he is only one of a long line of people employed elsewhere in the organisation – the service department, despatch, sales order office, production or anywhere – who could spoil a good relationship built-up with the customer.

A man working alone in this manner needs support and motivation so that his enthusiasm may be maintained and his knowledge and skills fully exploited. The best support he can have is the good supervision of senior management who have the ability to plan; to communicate; to effect control in line with the plan; to acknowledge and show appreciation, when appropriate, of the representative's work. At the heart of this facility to communicate and control is the plan.

The plan for the sales force must spring from the requirements of the overall marketing plan.[1] A typical flow of decision-making which fits in with corporate objectives is shown in Figure 8.1.

The size of the market and its structure in terms of geographical spread, the user industries involved, the channels employed or by size of customer,

FIGURE 8.1.

*Sales Deployment and Market Strategy*

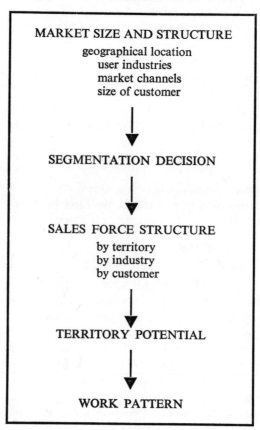

MARKET SIZE AND STRUCTURE
geographical location
user industries
market channels
size of customer

SEGMENTATION DECISION

SALES FORCE STRUCTURE
by territory
by industry
by customer

TERRITORY POTENTIAL

WORK PATTERN

[1]See chapter 1.

will provide information on which segments of the market should be covered. Also the structure of the sales force, by product, territory or customer, can be decided.

These are decisions of marketing strategy but on the assumption that these have been made, it is necessary to continue with a more tactical plan showing how the sales force can approach the task set.

## The Sales Plan

When considering territory potential in the development of a sales plan the following should be taken into account: identification of all existing and potential customers including competitors' customers and an estimation of the annual consumption/purchasing power. This information to be built up through marketing research, observation in the field, recommendation, contact with customers and prospects, trade directories and trade journals.

### Targets

These must be realistically based on territory potential, but most important, they must be explained fully to the representative. How based; how calculated. There should be no mystery nor divine law laid down from above. A 'grass roots' involvement in which the opinion of the sales representative is combined with head office calculations will result in a more efficient sales team.

This fact seems so obvious and yet some senior managers keep their target cards close to their chests.

### Work Pattern

First there is the application of the '*80/20 rule*' which reflects the concentration of up to 80 per cent of business activity in 20 per cent of the firms in an industry. Once the key customers have been identified, the time spent by the representative on the territory can be controlled through the division of the total time available into units of time, e.g. periods of 15 minutes. An assessment of the number of units required to cover each key customer can then be made. For example: key customer $A$, 8 units in a monthly cycle, or 24 hours per annum.

Such calculations may appear arbitrary in the everyday world of 'putting out fires' as and when they appear, but whatever the circumstances, it helps to keep representatives away from customers with little potential. It also provides a basis for a very simple calculation to check whether the representative can cope with the work plan established for him. When relating the number of time units allocated to the number of working days available during the year, the calculation showed incorporates an allowance for calling on prospective and potentially key customers. If no time is available for prospecting then the territory is too large.

## Qualities Required of the Salesman

Once properly directed in a physical sense, the next step is to ensure that the representative is not wasting time whilst with the customer by talking about things which buyers, and those members of a decision-making unit involved in buying, do not wish to hear.

Most of the people who buy have many other responsibilities and jobs to perform other than buying. The sales representative lives and breathes his product or service all the year round. Somehow, during the relatively short time allotted to him, he has to gain the attention of his listener, involve him and maintain his interest in such a manner that some positive action, such as placing an order, will eventually take place. In doing this the sales representative has to compete for the attention of a buying audience distracted by other, possibly more urgent, matters.

Personnel selectors have for long sought clues as to which personal features are likely to produce the best salesmen. Social scientists researching this area of recruitment at first found very little predictive significance in the social and psychological characteristics of salesmen. The characteristics for which there is no significant relationship with sales success include intelligence, stereotype 'sales' personality, age, education and level of sales activity.[1]

At first it would seem that there is no special characteristic which distinguishes the potentially good salesman, but when each of these factors of age, education, personality and level of activity are studied in relation to each other they provide a useful basis on which to compare the profiles of those who have been clearly seen to be successful or unsuccessful salesmen. In this way, the progressive sales recruiter can reduce the risk of taking on people who will completely fail when sent out to sell.

For those companies whose sales recruitment does not include the services of a social psychologist, there is one characteristic which can be relied upon to indicate an applicant's suitability for the selling task and that is 'customer compatibility'. But what is meant by customer compatibility in this sense? Surely it does not mean the representative, chameleon-like, has to change in appearance or even in clothing to match a swinging young design engineer one minute or the more responsible senior purchasing manager the next? Obviously not. The compatibility here refers to a mental compatibility or the ability to identify with the customer's environment and the problems encountered in that environment. This is no mean feat and it may appear that the qualities demanded of the sales representative are so high that insufficient applicants are available for such work. This, however, is true for all forms of employment in an

[1]S. N. Stevens, 'The Application of Social Science Findings to Selling and the Salesman', *Marketing and Administrative Action*, ed., S. H. Britt and H. W. Boyd, McGraw-Hill (New York, 1968).

economy which relies on growth through technical sophistication. The answer to the problem is to be found in training. The representative has to be 'taught' customer compatibility.

## Training Sales Representatives

Training is normally associated in the minds of management with the high overheads of company training premises, trainers and supporting staff, such as the investments made by the largest employer, the Civil Service, down to the fiftieth of the top fifty companies in the country. These organisations justify this expenditure through the large numbers of staff, of all types, who require training.

For the company seeking to contain the cost of training, there is the choice of either sending sales personnel to standard external courses run by specialist sales trainers, or of setting up an 'in-company' course (again normally with the assistance of a sales training specialist), to take advantage of tailoring the sales approach to the specific needs of the organisation, its products and the individuals to be trained. The first alternative is a known commodity which can be assessed and evaluated. The second, however, by definition, offers a variety of possible approaches and mixtures of content.

Sales representatives require regular training in the following key topics, in addition to a routine up-dating in company administrative procedures: product knowledge, application knowledge, product benefits, customer knowledge/purchasing patterns, competitor knowledge and sales techniques.

The advantage of the in-company tailored course is that learning sales techniques can be combined in a fully credible and realistic manner with the essential product and trade knowledge. The extent of product and application training must vary with the experience of the representatives concerned with the designated sales plan but, whatever the level, two basic principles should be covered, namely that all purchasing is problem-solving and all purchasing is risk-taking.

If this is accepted, the training should emphasise the need to discover and understand customer problems, to be aware of the associated risks in a buyer's mind and to learn how to reduce those risks.

## A Sales Training Framework

Companies planning their own in-company sales training will consider a number of ways of incorporating these concepts of problem-solving and risk-taking, but the following will provide a framework for such a programme:

- The role of selling in the marketing mix.

- Exercise in the comparison of product/service features and benefits.

● Discussion of the sales sequence.

● Listing of ways of creating interest.

● Listing of objections and their classification.

● Role playing with possible objections.

● Examinations of how objections are overcome.

● Technique of closing the sale.

● Role playing to incorporate creating interest, overcoming objection and closing the sale.

● Course review and discussion.

This series of topics provides an outline for a three to five day course using live situations and examples acceptable to the sales representatives involved and offering ample opportunity for the use of participative techniques on which real learning is based.

### Incorporating Research Findings

Money is wasted every time a sales training course is run by lecturers who fail to update their material with information culled from the continuing research into purchasing behaviour, and yet the results of this research form an important part of low-cost sales development.

The majority of the early work in the industrial field, for example, concentrated on the topics of rational versus irrational behaviour. One school of thought would continue to propound that the buyers in organisations act rationally; the other, that such buyers were open to persuasion through all the normal human emotions. As more and more evidence was provided of both apparently rational and obviously irrational actions, it became clear that the answer was elsewhere. The solution was to be found eventually in the fundamental concept of purchasing as risk-taking. The concept states that:[1] 'consumer behaviour involves risk in the sense that any action of a consumer will produce consequences which he cannot anticipate with anything approaching certainty', and also that: 'consumers characteristically develop decision strategies and ways of reducing risk that enable them to act with relative confidence and ease in situations where their information is inadequate and the consequences of their action are in some meaningful sense incalculable.'

A further step forward in research was made in the 1960s with the 'How Industry Buys' surveys in the United States, Canada and the United

---

[1] R. A. Baver, 'Consumer Behaviour as Risk-Taking', Proceedings 43rd Conference American Marketing Association (Chicago, 1960).

Kingdom. These studies quantified the involvement of the various members of the decision-making unit numbering up to six or seven different departments such as production, finance, sales, purchasing, or the board itself, who together are responsible for buying decisions.

The acceptance of the buyer as only one of a group of executives involved in the decision to purchase plant equipment, materials and components, brought the research effort nearer to the everyday problems of the industrial marketing practitioner faced with the task of reaching a number of technical, financial and commercial personnel operating at different levels of management and, at times, inaccessible to the sales engineer or representative.

Further research was required, however, to unravel the apparent paradox of the increasing acceptance of the DMU principle of shared decision-taking which reduces the relative importance of the designated buyer at a time when the skill and professionalism of purchasing were gaining more recognition in company management. This came with the research into purchasing as a process continuing through a number of relatively clearly defined buying stages.[1] This work was expanded in the United Kingdom to show how the composition of the decision-making unit varies between the buying stages and for different types of purchase, in particular those new to the company, those which could be considered as regular repeat purchases and those where a regular supplier is changed for a new supplier.[2]

Figure 8.2. shows a typical flow of decision-making for the purchase of a product new to a company and can be used in sales training, for example, to provoke discussion of the stages and personnel encounters by the participants in their contact with customers.

The practising sales manager has little time in his busy routine to keep abreast of the increasing amount of research data now becoming available. Even worse, his administrative load may be so heavy that he cannot keep in touch with the day-to-day problems faced by his own sales representatives. In these circumstances, there is the possibility that sales training courses may simply become 'repeat purchases' covering the same ground year in, year out, without modification.

This is not quite so alarming as it may first appear, as there are fundamental concepts (e.g. how will it benefit me?) which need to be covered in sales courses, and which are as true today as they were when men first began to barter between themselves. But these fundamental concepts have to be applied in a changing world and recognition can be given to these changes through a fresh look at the buying process.

[1] P. J. Robinson *et al*, *Industrial Buying and Creative Marketing*, Allyn & Bacon (Boston, Mass., 1967).
[2] Gordon Brand, *The Industrial Buying Decision*, Associated Business Programmes (London, 1972).

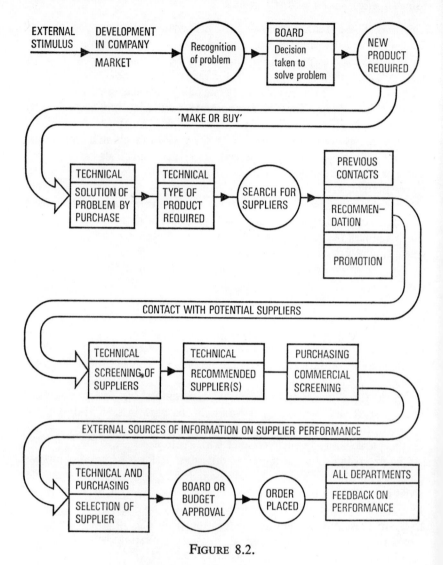

FIGURE 8.2.

*The Industrial Buying Decision*

### Sales Research and Sales Training

The relation between the research knowledge and the sales approach may at first look too remote for practical application in the 'knock-about' of a role-playing sales training course, but nevertheless a link may be made. Figure 8.3. lists on one side the research finding based on the results of far reaching, well-conducted surveys and, on the other, the corresponding sales situation which the more traditional sales training courses normally cover. An examination of these two lists will provide ideas for material to be used in the tailor-made, in-company course referred to above.

FIGURE 8.3.

*Relation of Research Knowledge to the Sales Approach*

| Research Knowledge | Sales Approach |
|---|---|
| DMU concept<br>TASK concept | Ask questions<br>Listen to find out what is relevant to each DMU member |
| New Purchase—'information hunger'<br>Change Supplier—commercial dissatisfaction<br>Repeat Purchase—preferred list | — provide information<br><br>— concentrate on commercial factors<br>— regular calling |
| COMMUNICATIONS Technical Buyer<br>EFFECTS     Non-Technical Buyer | — Stress technical 'image'<br>— Good sales presentation |
| ALL PURCHASING IS RISK-TAKING<br><br><br><br>INERTIA | Reduce risk through *validated* information<br>Provide outside references<br>Provide guarantees of competence<br>Carry out promises<br>Encourage visits to other customer installation<br>Encourage favourable WOM contact Sell the Benefits |
| BUYER AS STATUS SEEKER | Keep Buyer informed of progress with Technical Decision taken |
| INCREASE POWER/INFLUENCE OF PROFESSIONAL BUYER | Relate benefits to customer industry problems. Knowledge of customer markets<br>Stress of 'profit centre' aspect of purchasing role |

During this chapter a view has been given of an approach to the development of a sales force which is consistent with the marketing concept. The planning procedures referred to, which are applicable to both a large and small sales force, require thought and adaptation but, in themselves, very little expenditure. The direction and content of the sales training programmes similarly need no higher expenditure than that required for the traditional training regularly conducted throughout the country.

**The Future**

The principles of selling remain constant. The marketing skills employing those principles thrive, however, in periods of change and we cannot expect the operation of the sales function within the marketing mix to survive unchanged through periods of supply shortages, inflationary interest rates and high labour costs.

The cost of personal selling (estimated in 1974 to average £6,650 per annum for a manufacturer's representative calling on retailers) can be cut by reducing the time spent with unprofitable customers and by an evaluation of the logistics of journey patterns requiring extended mileage and/or hotel expenses.

The high cost of motoring is likely to force companies to explore other, less expensive, means of communicating with customers. In times of restricted economic growth personal selling effort will be concentrated even more on the larger VIP customers and sales expertise will be assisted by a greater understanding of the intricacies of pricing and other financial aspects of the sales deal.

Certain food manufacturers, in the front line of market change, have reacted to the high cost of selling to grocery outlets by contracting the total sales function to food brokers. In the United States, brokers account for 60 per cent of the sales to grocery outlets. The potential for the extension of this 'commando' or sales launch task force selling to a regular contractual responsibility is likely to grow in the United Kingdom as companies strive to reduce selling overheads and improve the flexibility of their selling effort.

A further alternative which should be considered by the small budget marketeer is telephone selling. Used more for order taking than initial sales contact telephone selling has expanded as dialling aids have facilitated the use of the telephone and the cost savings that can occur through higher productivity have become more widely appreciated.

Mail order selling, well developed in consumer goods marketing, is likely to receive greater attention in the industrial goods field particularly where the number of potential purchasers is large and the value of individual orders is low. Many publishers sell business books by this technique and there are a host of other products which could be handled in the same way.

## CHECKLIST

● What is the present size of the sales force and how is it deployed?

● Is it necessary to employ an 'in-house' sales team or can the sales function be sub-contracted?

- What proportion of sales are achieved through direct representation as opposed to other methods?

- What are the average sales per representative and how does this compare with the performance of similar companies?

- What type of salesman and selling effort is required? Are present salesmen too good or inadequate for the task?

- Has the sales force been given precise objectives and directives?

- Who is responsible for sales planning and control? Is the sales force centrally controlled?

- Has the structure of the market been studied to provide information on which to base the sales organisation?

- Has a detailed sales plan been developed?

- Is each representative covering the largest manageable sales territory?

- What incentives exist to maximise orders gained by salesmen?

- What support services exist to maximise the efficiency of the sales force?

- What steps are taken to ensure that salesmen meet the key decision-makers and that the number of wasted calls is minimised?

CHAPTER 9

# Exporting on a Small Budget

BY SIMON HODGSON

The common attitude that export is additional to the main stream of business continues to exist and supports the widely held opinion that exports are less profitable than home markets, expensive to obtain and of benefit to the exporter principally for the reason that they help to take up spare capacity in times of slack home demand. That is tantamount to saying that if profit were the only motive, nobody would export. Indeed, many companies that have a mild or more strongly expressed regret of their commitment to export markets are likely to be ones who have not set clearly defined objectives in advance.

The reasons for this attitude are quite understandable, but spring from a fundamental and common cause – that of not defining precisely where the best opportunities lie, and then pursuing these limited opportunities with the same single-mindedness that is applied to home markets. Exporting, then, becomes a poor relation of the marketing family of functions, producing below-average profit results and above-average frustration in those involved.

Successive British Governments have devised their own special provisions for encouraging exports, with varying degrees of success. The Queen's Award to Industry, though somewhat paternal in concept is, as a scheme, preferable to the rather depressing slogan 'export or die' in fashion some years ago. The nation, however, has as a whole always been aware of the vital role of exporting in maintaining and increasing its overall wealth, international competitiveness and living standards. It is all the more curious to reflect that there are so many companies who do not export at all, or who only sell minute proportions of their output overseas. Even more interesting is to examine the way in which many highly successful exporting industries achieve their results, often with very small budgets. For example, Britain's small boat-building industry, which is highly fragmented and consists of many very small firms, has been highly success-ful in export markets despite the small average size of these companies.

Caravan manufacturing during the 1960s was another relatively fragmented industry which also achieved a very high volume of export business. As a result, the industry is now one in which export promotional budgets, starting from small beginnings, are now running at unprecedentedly high levels.

At the other end of the scale there are still many private and publicly owned companies of substantial size which undertake little or no exporting. Many multi-national companies with establishments in Britain are prevented by their parent companies from exporting to some of the more lucrative export territories, while others are prevented by political or commercial restrictions from trading overseas. Yet there are companies, especially those serving traditionally declining markets which manage to export their products, despite the most meagre export efforts, usually as a result of long-standing relationships with local agents, often set up in the early days of the manufacturer's existence. Carbon pile regulators, a steadily declining market, find substantial export sales in long-life original equipment, such as the fishing vessels and locomotives into which they are incorporated, as a replacement market. The budgets necessary for selling these products are minimal.

Not all companies however, are in a position to export successfully on a small budget. By the nature of their business many companies, particularly manufacturers of consumer products such as detergents, confectionery, foods and, in some cases, cosmetics, in almost all industrialised countries, face a competitive market situation which requires substantial budgets for advertising, distribution, market research and all other related marketing activities if the local competition is to be met on its own terms. However once international marketing is established there are economies to be made, even if the scale of the expenditure is higher than purely national marketing effort. The automobile industry has found the cost of designing and promoting a single model for a number of different markets, such as the Ford Capri for the British and German markets, an important way of rationalising marketing as well as production costs.

There is, however, a very large number of companies whose products are sold to markets where large marketing budgets are not necessary. Many industrial products fall into this category and, indeed, a substantial number of consumer products are also effectively marketed overseas on small budgets.

## The Concept of the Unique Product

Unique products, by definition, are specialised in one form or another. They may be specialised because of their unusual design, such as Danish furniture, Norwegian sweaters or Irish floor coverings; they may be specialised because of their unusual function or performance, such as vehicle radar, animal feed formulation computers or continuous gas chromatographs; they may be specialised because of the high quality of manufacture, such as Swiss chronometers or British racing dinghies for the sailing enthusiasts, or they may be specialised because of their appeal to a narrow but easily defined sector of the market, such as paints for the model builder, or hair-springs for industrial instruments.

In such cases the products have a unique selling proposition (USP) which should form the basis of market planning and promotion and which, while not in itself a guarantee of success, is nevertheless a *sine qua non* for companies wishing to export them on a small budget.

Another category of products for which low budget exporting is possible includes all items which, because of favourable production conditions at home, have a price advantage in international markets. The current success of the Italian colour printer and French domestic glassware can be explained in these terms. In such markets, a high degree of customer service is not necessary and the most significant factor distinguishing suppliers is commercial – price and delivery. Thus those countries where costs structures are particularly favourable and which have established themselves for long production runs at low unit prices can export with comparative ease, and hence with low promotional budgets. Footwear from Hong Kong and finished woodwork from Taiwan are examples where exporting takes place with a minimal marketing budget. The success of suppliers in such markets depends largely on appropriately selected local importing agents overseas.

The common denominator to all products which can be exported successfully with small budgetary resources is thus one of uniqueness in the market place – uniqueness of quality, of style, of performance, of distribution method – or of price where the appropriate cost structure of the exporting country allows it. Without a unique customer benefit, the exporter joins a competitive rat race and with small export marketing budgets he is destined to remain among the supplying 'also rans' as he finds himself competing with local manufacturers who are well established in their own markets and are likely themselves to be indulging in substantial promotional activities.

The concept of uniqueness has, however, an additional dimension since what is unique in one market may not be unique in another. The new and currently fashionable natural wood finishes for certain furniture products in Germany have not been widely accepted in Britain and would in the present state of market consciousness find relatively little demand in France, whereas Italy has provided an interesting market opportunity for German manufacturers. The first of the key activities for the successful exporter within limited budgets available is, therefore, to identify those markets where his product is likely to have a unique selling proposition and which will offer him the most favourable opportunities for the least cost.

**Assessing Alternative Markets**

In establishing which markets offer the best potential for his products the exporter faces a bewildering variety of choice, and this is particularly so for the 'first time' exporter or the company with only a small budget available. Should he direct his activities to the industrialised countries where competition will be greater, but where unique products are better understood and where information channels are better established? Or would he be more successful breaking new ground in the less developed territories where the long-term benefits may be greater? Is it likely to be more profitable to supply a small potential market and achieve a high unit profit, or a high volume, more competitive, market? Is the product likely to need expensive modification for the target markets? These, and a host of other questions, pose themselves as soon as exporting is considered.

For the exporter with a small budget, indeed even for the experienced exporter seeking to enter new markets, selecting the most suitable markets is the crucial and often most difficult decision he has to take. All too often formalised exporting emerges by accident, resulting from a trickle of intermittent enquiries which develop into a more regular stream if the product has proven unique properties. A small export organisation emerges, often working part-time and based in the home territory. When the volume of exports proves sufficient, a decision is taken to constitute the growing operation as a fully operational export department. In this sequence accident has taken the place of decision but, although the results may prove profitable and in every way beneficial to the company, the owners are left with the nagging question of whether the market or markets they are exporting to are indeed the best and most profitable ones they could be supplying. What is needed is an assessment of the possible alternatives so that a clear plan of action can be formulated. This may be done by means of an inexpensive but effective market research study.[1]

Information on export markets is essential for making the initial decisions which will so vitally affect the company's resulting performance. The chapter concerning market research on a small budget has discussed the kind of data which can be generated with limited resources and, in the case of export market research, particular attention should be paid to sources which are available at home if expensive overseas travel is to be minimised. Fortunately there has been a substantial improvement in the quality and accuracy of data available which has made the preliminary examination of export opportunities a far less expensive activity than has been the case hitherto.

As a result of the greater reliability of published data it is normal for

[1]See chapter 5 ('Marketing Research on a Small Budget'). Readers should note that under certain conditions grants covering 30–50 per cent research costs for export studies are available from the British Overseas Trade Board.

the manager assessing export opportunities to undertake research in two separate, but connected phases. The first phase provides an *overview* of the market situation, covering the economic, competitive and, where appropriate, the political climate in each prospective country, together with as much specific information on the structure and size of the market as is obtainable without involving expensive fieldwork. The aim of this first phase is to obtain comprehensive and, most important, directly comparable information on each alternative market so that at the end the alternative countries can be placed in order of priority according to criteria previously identified as indicative of the market potential.

Having thus identified which products and markets are likely to prove most attractive, then a more detailed survey, involving local field research, is undertaken to refine or generate statistical data on the market in question, and to obtain information on users' unfulfilled needs, their opinions of existing products and suppliers and on their purchasing practices. The second phase of the research will be geared to providing information on which to base a decision on the best method of entry to the market, the promotional methods and media which should be used for optimum cost-effectiveness, the most suitable agent or joint-venture partner, the timing of market entry, the pricing policies of competitors and the other crucial data necessary for realistic objective setting and market planning.

Each individual product or market situation requires its own approach. Research appropriate for, say, industrial filters would not apply to high quality confectionery. However, the two following examples illustrate the kind of two-phased research approach which might be undertaken to identify export opportunities.

In a study of export markets for tape cassettes and cartridges the indicators used for comparing the size of potential market included the volume of output, exports and imports of magnetic tape, the number and average size of musical recording companies, *per capita* disposable income estimates related to population, price levels of cassette and cartridge players, extent of advertising by record player manufacturers and ownership of electrical items such as radio, television and car radios.

Information on these factors was quite simply and cheaply generated from the trade press, trade associations and publications readily available in good commercial libraries, such as the City Business Library, or the respective countries' embassies in Britain.

A similar approach applied to the demand in export markets for a specialist form of wire rope might include examination of the following information on the market: general statistics on the volume and trends in production, imports and exports of all types of wire rope in as much detail as available from published sources, the number and size of existing manufacturers, the number and location of their service depots, size growth trends and location of user industries, price information and border tariffs and profitability of existing manufacturers.

Such information is again readily available from published sources and no expensive field research should be required. In addition, a thorough analysis of the range of products available from existing manufacturers, drawn from their catalogues, will enable the manufacturer with limited funds for product development or modification to assess where the market gap lies.

Each of the examples has a common feature which is also common to most industrial markets, that is that statistical data on the precise market in question is insufficiently obtained to enable strategic and tactical decisions to be taken. As a result a degree of interpretation of the data is required which compensates for not having market information in the exact form required. In each case the key factors affecting the potential market to the manufacturers are the overall size of the market for his product, the rate of growth of the demand, the extent and nature of competition, the structure and nature of the end user industries (or distribution for consumer products) and compatibility with existing markets.

In most industrial markets a full-scale study is often necessary to obtain refined information with detailed breakdowns of the size of the market so that in an overview it is necessary to locate and analyse information on factors which may not give direct indication of the actual size of demand for the product but which will provide an order of magnitude and, particularly, a scale for inter-country comparison which is sufficiently accurate for placing a priority order on alternative markets.

It is normal at the end of an export market overview to establish a rating or screening process in order to make a reasoned and balanced assessment of each market. Management experience will indicate whether a diverse or concentrated distribution of users favours their kind of business, whether the unique aspects of their product have special benefits to different sectors of the market, what the company turnover and profit objectives are, and what special factors need to be taken into account when establishing the rating or screening criteria.

Some markets may reject themselves early in the process for specific reasons; for example, there may be legal restrictions which emerge during the research process, or technical standards which cannot be met without major product redesign. In such circumstances a totally new approach is required and it will be necessary to postpone any plans for market entry until a later date. Thus the overview research will result in a priority order of export opportunities with information presented either diagrammatically or in tabular and text format.

The total cost of such a screening process can be as low as a few hundred pounds, especially if the executive carrying out the research is able to do so in spare moments as an addition to his normal duties. At worst he will need to spend a few weeks full-time on the study, while at best he may be able to use an intelligent secretary, particularly if she has some language capability, to do much of the initial information-gathering, leaving him to analyse and interpret the data. The next stage is a full and open discussion with marketing and general management to agree which markets, based on the research findings to date, offer the most attractive opportunities. Following this decision a further, more detailed research programme may be necessary specifically for planning market entry and development strategy.

Just how the second phase research can be most effectively and cheaply carried out will depend on the nature of the product, the executive time and resources available, the extent of language capability, knowledge of local trading practices and the need for confidentiality. First the make or buy decision has to be taken. The real cost of overseas field research is never small although by conducting as much as possible of the study internally the apparent cost may seem less. A wide variety of alternatives is available, ranging from commissioning a local agency, with the attendant problems of how to locate and select the best and brief them unambiguously, to undertaking the project entirely internally, with possible time, skills, and confidentiality disadvantages. The most effective method is undoubtedly to commission a United Kingdom agency with substantial overseas skills and experience. An alternative method is to conduct the study internally and to sub-contract the field research to a local interview field force experienced in the market under investigation. A 'combined' approach such as this can, however, only be carried out in the developed industrial world where such field forces are now well established.

In deciding how best to undertake detailed research in overseas markets one of the major considerations is likely to be the question of language. Those whose foreign language capacity is limited to school French are unlikely to be successful either in their research or selling, even in France. The ideal situation, so rarely achievable in practice, is to use researchers or salesmen who are bilingual and who fully understand the different cultures, values and business practices of the countries concerned. However, fluency in the local language is not always essential although it is an advantage if only to show courtesy to the customer. The Englishman is still noted for his 'reserve' in learning new languages and foreigners have considerable respect for a genuine effort by the Englishman to speak their language, even if the bulk of the discussion eventually takes place in English.

Senior management in large companies of most industrialised nations are quite accustomed to speaking English in business, so that if purchasing decisions are taken at this level, both research and selling can be effectively carried out in English. The lower down the management scale the purchasing decision occurs, the more likely the necessity to speak the local language. Thus the nature of the product itself decides the need to speak the language when researching or selling. For example a multi-million pound chemical plant can be sold, in most countries, with English as the basic language, whereas disposable small tools for metal-cutting machine tools would need to be sold in the native language of the customer, since the choice of supplier is often taken at shopfloor level.

As far as different countries are concerned, English is a practical business language in most Commonwealth countries, Scandinavia, Holland, Switzerland and sectors of industry in Western Germany, Italy and Austria. But local language capability is essential in France, Spain, the South American continent and less developed countries, particularly those with little or no traditional link with Britain.

## Alternative Exporting Methods

Once a decision has been taken to enter an export market the most appropriate method of making that entry must be chosen. Figure 9.1. shows the alternative methods of operation for companies in overseas markets ranging from personal direct selling to full-scale local manufacture and selling, the different methods of operation being arranged in order of increasing financial commitment to the market place. A breakpoint is made arbitrarily between the ownership of distribution channel and overseas local assembly since this is the point of which physical exporting becomes less significant and where the decision for major financial commitment is made.

As companies become increasingly committed to export markets they tend to gravitate up the scale. However, each individual new market requires careful analysis in order to decide at which point in this scale it is appropriate for the exporter to begin his operation. It is likely that companies exporting with a small budget will select one or other of the bottom four methods, since above this level major capital expenditure is required in order to set up the appropriate organisation.

The actual method selected will depend on a whole range of factors different for different products and marketing situations, but is likely to include the expected volume of business, user's need for personal advice or service, before or after sales, distribution systems normally used, transport costs of the product in relation to overall costs, language capabilities/knowledge of local trading conditions, the level of risk the exporter is prepared to take, the volume of funds available to developing export markets and pressures from government in the export and home markets. Market research and discussions will indicate which method is the best for individual circumstances.

- Direct Personal Selling

- Local Exclusive Agencies

- Joint Ventures

- Locally Owned Distribution Channels

------------------------------------------------

- Assembly of Product in Overseas Markets

- Full Scale Local Manufacture

INCREASING COMMITMENT TO OVERSEAS MARKET

FIGURE 9.1.

*Alternative Methods of Marketing Overseas*

*Direct Personal Selling*

This form of promotion can be extremely successful, particularly where the exporter has a small number of large potential customers or where his customers can, for one reason or another, be very clearly defined. Companies selling, for example, to the coal mining industry can, with negligible expenditure of time and money, identify their prospect companies with great ease through the appropriate trade directories, trade associations or chambers of commerce. The manufacturer with a product conferring unique benefits to the coal mining industry would thus find himself in a position to export with a small personal selling budget simply because the extent of his commitment would be the cost of overseas visits to the few target prospects.

The rewards resulting from such a small time and cost expenditure could, of course, be enormous given the vast purchasing power of coal mining companies.

Any product which requires a high degree of pre-sales technical advice, and particularly those designed for specific markets, such as analogue computers for chemical formulation or gas chromatographs for essential oil separation, need to be marketed overseas with a strong emphasis on personal selling. However, where markets become ill-defined, where the distribution channels are complex or where the prospects are located within manufacturing or commercial organisations, the very fragmentation of customer outlets places a heavy burden in time and cost on the supplier if personal selling is undertaken direct from the manufacturing country.

## Local Exclusive Agencies

The use of local exclusive agencies is one of the most important traditional methods of setting up an organisation to sell overseas and, indeed, in most industries this method is likely to remain the most important. Many such agencies are highly successful for both themselves and their principals, with an ever-increasing awareness of the whole marketing function by both agents and their suppliers. It is to be expected that such exclusive arrangements will flourish on an increasingly wide basis.

Nevertheless, there are many local agencies of this type which are not acting in the best interest of their principals, not out of dishonesty on the part of the agent but because of the simple fact that the real interests of the agent so rarely coincide precisely with those of his principal. After all, the agent 'sells what sells' and probably acts for a large number of manufacturers. If his principal's product is not the 'star of the show' then it will not get 'star' treatment. The facts are as simple as that.

Careful market research beforehand can, however, help to pinpoint those agencies which are most successful in the market place and also those whose interests are most likely to coincide with those of the principal.

The British machine tool industry, notorious in the past for a proliferation of overseas agents, has found to its cost in recent years that the real needs of their overseas agents have been met by other products. As a result, the agent's performance has deteriorated in the market place and similar products made by foreign competitive manufacturers have gained ground. Research conducted in Denmark has shown, for example, that West German machine tool manufacturers have been more successful in recent years than their British counterparts in selecting and motivating effective local agents in that country,[1] by providing products and services which met the agencies' needs more effectively.

The tragedy in such a situation is that the principal usually perceives the problem only when it is too late to take an effective counter-action. The situation develops because of lack of control and indeed often the lack of knowledge of the marketing activities of the agent and, more important, the total absence of market feed-back through the agent to the principal. The key to successful exporting through local agents lies, therefore, in

[1]*The Market for Metal Working Machine Tools in Denmark,* BNEC Export Council for Europe, 1971.

developing as quickly as possible a close understanding of the end customer's particular needs, agreeing realistic sales targets with the agent,
maintaining close contact with the necessary back-up services which
ensure a smooth administration and insisting on an effective feed-back
of market information.

It is surprising how many manufacturers expect the sales agent to
operate with the minimum of control and reporting procedures, but who
would nevertheless be aghast at the suggestion that such a lack of control
be applied to their own selling force in their home market.

Much has been said and written about exporting through agents and
the management activities necessary for success. The conclusion usually
drawn is that expensive market research, coupled with large promotional
sums, is necessary. However, experience in researching a wide variety of
overseas market has clearly indicated that above-average success lies not
in the simple fact of 'appointing an agent' and then motivating him to
sell effectively, but in identifying the agent whose long and short-term
interests closely accord with those of the principal, and then negotiating
terms and the most appropriate methods of operation. When negotiating
with a new principal an overseas agent holds the joker and all four aces
in his hand, since he has the one prime advantage of having detailed
'grass roots' experience in the market place. Even the most realistic agent
cannot fail to be optimistic in his negotiations with a new principal if his
own interests are best served by offering his customers a broad product
line. Of course the principal will negotiate minimum sales levels and other
criteria for 'ensuring' the success of the agency, but no guarantees yet
devised make up for the time, energy and cost dissipated in making good
the agent's lack of performance when it is too late.

Ideally, the agency approach to exporting should be considered as a
transitional stage and not as an end in itself. The principal establishes
his foothold in a new market in this way, but it is important that plans
should be laid for development in that market which will ensure that the
agency will be fully developed, and possibly ultimately replaced by a more
direct involvement in the market when the volume of business or trading
conditions warrants such a move.

*Joint Ventures*

A joint venture between two appropriate partners can be an extremely
effective method of exploiting export opportunities. The initial costs of
setting up the joint venture as far as the basic capital requirements are
concerned can be as large or as small as the two partners require, and as
are jointly deemed appropriate for the market concerned. Although not
specifically geared to exploiting export markets, the AA-Reader's Digest
joint operation has been one of the most successful in its field, capitalising
on the joint strengths of the two organisations. However size alone is no

guarantee of success in a joint venture, as the Dunlop-Pirelli venture has recently shown.

Joint venture usually implies two or occasionally more partners, probably though not necessarily from separate countries, forming a distinct jointly-owned and controlled organisation to combine the complementary skills of the two partners. The advantage of such an operation over the exclusive sales agency is that there is a stronger degree of mutual commitment to the objectives of the new company than is the case within an agency system.

The initial capital requirements of the company, however small, tend to draw out a level of commitment from the partners which ensures a greater degree of success than is normally to be expected from agency arrangements. However, experience has indicated in the past that such ventures rarely succeed in the long-term unless one partner holds the ultimate control of the operation. Joint ventures on a fifty-fifty ownership basis start out with a severe handicap in terms of control, particularly in national operations where partisan emotion can so drastically interfere with business decisions. Much depends on the personalities involved and which partner takes the controlling ownership. In the absence of such personality factors, it is probably more appropriate for the partner with the strongest marketing skills to take the lead (in each country) in both industrial and consumer markets, since in times of rapid change it takes the strongest possible voice to ensure that changing customer requirements are appropriately met as they develop during the growth of the company.

Once again, the choice of the best possible partner is crucial to the long-term success of the operation. Too often the eventual partner is simply identified by chance acquaintance rather than being carefully selected from a number of candidates.

*Locally Owned Distribution Points*

Many companies entering new export territories find the long communication channels involved somewhat more problematic than an internal administrative difficulty. It is often a major problem for the exporter to demonstrate to his customers a genuine and firm commitment to the market unless he can do so by the existence of substantial locally-held assets.

The central distribution point provides this credibility, quite apart from the obvious additional benefits such as being able to provide speedy delivery and to obtain a valuable feed-back of market information. Further, by owning or leasing physical assets in the export territory there emerges an internal commitment to achieve an adequate return on these investments, and the whole exporting operation develops from being a peripheral activity to the exporting company to one with a keen cutting edge in the organisation as a whole. An additional factor in favour of acquisition of local distribution points is that it enables a relatively smooth transaction as trading volume grows from a simple warehousing activity to local assembly, and then to full-scale local manufacturing if this is appropriate in due course. However, if such an operation justifiably is no longer termed 'small budget exporting' it will nevertheless be the ultimate goal of many exporters who have genuine aspirations to establish themselves overseas.

An alternative form of joint venture, franchising, despite its somewhat tarnished image as a form of marketing operation, has been highly successful in certain fields. Franchising overseas normally requires a strong operation in the home markets (which may also operate on a franchise basis). The operation requires the franchisee and franchisor to split the costs – production, marketing and development, though not usually the operating costs – and also the profits on a formalised basis set out by the franchisor, in exchange for technical, managerial and other assistance in developing the business. The cost split between the two partners ensures that the budget required from each partner is smaller than would be the case on a 'go it alone' basis, but as a balancing factor the profit is also split.

The most striking examples of successful franchises are in food business, such as Wimpy Bars and more recently in the take-away field, Kentucky Fried Chicken. In non-food markets, Dyno-Rod drain clearing services have been highly successful as, indeed, have a number of contract cleaning services for industry. However, successful franchising operations are less common in industrial than in consumer goods markets where marketing plays such a key role in company operations.

**Promotion Overseas**

Previous chapters have discussed the whole field of sales and promotion within small budgets and have clearly shown how limited funds can be put to most effective use. Funds for these activities in export markets are likely to be even more limited since all too often the *overall* budget for exporting may be comparable in size to the budget for promotion alone in home markets. It is all the more important, therefore, that the limited effort is not in any way diluted or diverted from the central objective. For example, an export strategy may hinge around obtaining a hard core of key prestigious customers in the first six months of operation as a basis for building a highly prestigious image. In such circumstances initial trade press advertising would be wasted, even though it could be effective in building the required image once the target customers have been success-fully won.

Those exporting industrial goods overseas may find it possible, though not always advisable, to carry out their own promotion in overseas markets. In such cases product-literature (well presented and accurately translated) is likely to be the most cost-effective combination of promotional activities given the relatively small share of the market that is inevitably being sought.

The promotion of consumer goods in export markets is more problematic. In general, the comments made in chapter 7 are equally relevant in all industrialised countries but obviously the media vary in the services they offer and the target audiences differ in sophistication. The selection of a local agency or partner should therefore take into account their ability to guide, or even undertake, the necessary promotional activities without requiring the deployment of excessive resources. Direct mail addressed personally to the decision-makers by name can also be effective, especially if the 'message' has an arresting and even gimmicky content to it. In many markets the cost of obtaining the names of specific target recipients may be too high to be justifiable, but in certain instances the names are published in easily obtainable directories such as those published by Kompass and Dun & Bradstreet. Response rates to direct mail vary considerably but can be as high as 40 per cent for personally addressed letters. For high unit value products, figures as low as 1–2 per cent make this method of promotion attractive, so direct mail cannot be readily discarded from the exporter's promotional mix.

**Overseas Visits**

At some point, either during the assessment of export opportunities or the evaluation of the various methods of entering export markets, the potential exporter must visit the markets in which he is interested. For small marketing organisations this can itself be a major expense item requiring careful thought and planning if the investment is not to be wasted. The problem is particularly acute in the case of long distance markets which are not only expensive to visit, but also more difficult to communicate with on a regular basis. For this reason, the first-time exporter is well-advised to give higher priority to the nearest markets and to broaden his geographical horizons only as he gains experience and the cash flow from export sales builds up.

For the first visits overseas there are several methods of minimising the costs that will be incurred. The most obvious are the various group travel schemes that are organised by Governments, local chambers of commerce and a number of private sponsors. These are the business equivalent to package tours and provide set itineraries from which each participant may make his own departures to cover his special interests. Official visits may receive a grant which subsidises the cost of participating, and privately organised trips take advantage of special airline and hotel rates. The exporter who has no desire to tie himself to a set routine should still seek out the special discounts that are offered by airlines for advance and last minute bookings and round trips. Time invested in locating a knowledgeable travel agent will not be wasted.

While few business travellers will admit that they have time to spare on their journeys this is rarely the case. There is often time available which can be employed profitably for acquaintances and colleagues, in exchange for a contribution towards the travel costs. In fact the would-be exporter should himself seek to locate people who travel to the areas of interest and would be capable of obtaining information or making preliminary contacts. Though slightly less efficient, it is considerably cheaper than numerous abortive trips and if there are any doubts a special trip can always be undertaken. As the export programme develops substantial amounts of travelling may be required to administer the business. This, too, should be used to extend the export marketing effort. It is far less costly to extend a trip than to undertake one specially and client-servicing visits should provide a vehicle for making new marketing contacts. In this way the export marketing effort can be allowed to snowball to the ultimate profit of the company.

Finally, it is extremely easy to waste time on an overseas trip. The common causes of problems are insufficient preparation of travel routines so that time is wasted booking tickets and hotels, failure to contact those to be visited in advance, overcrowded travel schedules leading to hurried and missed meetings, inadequate knowledge of the countries and local trading conditions, and failure to advise embassy and consular staff of the visit so that they can provide appropriate local assistance.

Each of these can lead to losses in time, missed opportunities and a poor result from the trip. Planning is essential even to the extent of ensuring that the health of the traveller is up to the physical demands that will be placed on him.[1]

### Summary of the Critical Factors for Success in Exporting

The key to successful exporting lies in:

- Identifying which export markets offer the best opportunities as a result of the unique customer benefits conferred by the product.

- Establishing clear objectives and targets for business, together with the appropriate information systems to measure how actual performance compares with the targets.

- Making a careful assessment of the alternative methods of operation in the specified markets.

[1]A useful guide to the mechanics of exporting is *Getting Started in Export Trade*, published by International Trade Centre UNCTAD/GATT (Geneva, 1970).

- If relevant, selecting the most suitable business partners (e.g. local sales agency, joint venture partners.)

- Providing the essential support services for effective marketing.

- Obtaining continuous market information feed-back for future objectives setting and policy-making.

Each one of these steps can be a substantial exercise, and unless the product or service itself has a unique aspect to it then the actual process of exporting is likely to be a costly one.

If no markets exist for your company's product although it displays strong unique features, then exporting will only be successful if supported by substantial promotional budgets. Thus with a specific range of products the first questions which arise are: can we export? if so to which countries and in what quantities? what will be the associated costs? None of these questions can be answered without detailed information on the markets which form the potential targets, and the research itself will clearly indicate whether exporting can take place within a specific budgetary framework.

If the market situation revealed by the research indicates that a new supplier cannot readily achieve a unique position then it may be wiser to abandon any thoughts of exporting, and devote the money to other projects in the company which will increase the competitiveness, and hence the ability to export more effectively at a later date.

Research has always been and will continue to be the basis on which export marketing decisions are most effectively taken. 'Hunch' is a great deal cheaper, provided it derives from the right person, but the built-in experience necessary for successful 'hunch' decisions is rarely, if ever, available to the exporter in the same measure as it is available in the home market.

## CHECKLIST

- What unique features do the products possess that would facilitate penetration of export markets?

- How many overseas countries can the export marketing effort cover with the resources available?

- Have the export markets been studied to show which offer the greatest potential and are best suited to the company's products?

- Have the characteristics of the export markets been studied, and is the export marketing effort geared to prevailing market conditions?

- Will the profit yield from export sales justify the effort involved?

● Which methods of overseas representation are best suited to the volume of sales likely to be achieved and the future plans of the company?

● Have potential business partners in each market been identified and evaluated?

● What support services are available to those engaging in the export effort?

# CHAPTER 10

# *Organising for Marketing on a Small Budget*

By Richard Skinner

The structure of most companies has evolved pragmatically in response to business pressures rather than through the application of an enduring master plan. If one such pressure has been towards a marketing approach aimed at identifying and satisfying customer needs at a profit, this might be expected to be revealed in the organisational structure of successful marketing companies. It is, of course, unlikely that ready-made models will be found which a company with limited resources might adopt as they stand, but some indications at least may be obtained from the experience of others. The problem lies in identifying this experience for what it really is.

A study of the organisation charts which fill the pages of marketing manuals does little to help. The labels and lines on the chart are quite inadequate to reflect the complicated interrelationships between the individuals concerned, and the picture given is at best a compromise between what actually happens and what the managing director would like to believe is happening. Detailed schedules of responsibilities can prove more useful but, before examining these, it is worthwhile taking a fresh look at the concept of marketing, to see how it could be applied in practice by a company requiring full value for every penny of additional expense.

Traditionally, the functions involved in a business can be shown as follows:

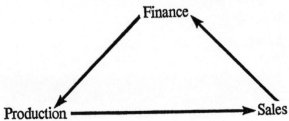

The relationship between these three functions has been considered as a balance of power, which if adjusted correctly, brings success, and if pushed out of alignment, causes problems. The marketing concept finds no easy entry into this closed circle unless it is regarded merely as a synonym for sales. Such a solution may be painless, since the balance can then remain undisturbed, but for marketing to be effective, a complete reappraisal of the relationships between functions is necessary, and the whole notion of a balance of power between departments with differing interests needs to be called into question.

It will be clear from the preceding chapters that the marketing approach impinges on all sections of a company. Whether or not specialist personnel are employed, the whole company must be geared to identifying and satisfying customer needs for marketing to produce opportunities for additional profit. From this it follows that the backing of senior management is required – marketing is not something that can be brought in at a low level in the hope that the idea will catch on. It is also clear that marketing is in some sense a planning and co-ordinating function, whatever specialised techniques are employed in given instances. Its role has to be accepted by other departments, and this has implications when it comes to defining marketing tasks more precisely. The planning function may be considered as part of the role previously played by the managing director, now delegated to someone with more time to handle in detail the issues involved. It is, however, a customer-oriented function, and in practice it is associated with other customer-oriented functions such as selling or advertising. These are normally considered straightforward line responsibilities and it is not easy to sustain a dual role involving planning on behalf of the company as a whole and a clear-cut responsibility for, say, obtaining an agreed number of orders over a stipulated period of time. It is around this duality of function that most of the organisational problems of marketing revolve.

This chapter will consider in turn the job of marketing, the assignment of specific responsibilities to individuals, sources of suitable personnel, selection techniques, career structures and methods of control. The problems of relating marketing to the activities of other departments will be considered and the rewards to be gained from effective organisation outlined, together with a summary of the managerial steps to be taken. The emphasis throughout will be on achieving results with the minimum additional staff.

## Marketing Functions

As it has developed, marketing has encompassed a variety of functions which may be classified under the headings of either planning or action. Figure 10.1. lists the most important of these. The action functions are those which are aimed directly at the customer and are intended in one way or another to communicate the company's message to him. Planning functions serve a more complex purpose. They not only serve to set targets and give guidance to line management on the marketing side, but are also concerned with the co-ordination of the efforts of design engineers, production men and accountants in making the best use of the company's resources.

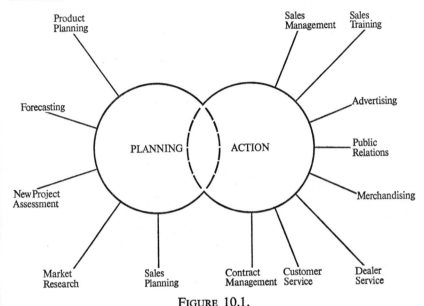

FIGURE 10.1.

*Marketing Functions*

### Separate or Combined?

Obviously, there must be a point at which action and planning functions are reconciled and decisions made on the plans to be adopted, and the most effective means of promoting them. In a very small company, all this may take place within the head of one man, the owner of the business. With growth, the marketing function as a whole may be delegated, although historically the first step has usually been to delegate only a part, and appoint a sales manager, leaving the important planning role still in the control of the owner or managing director. This leads to problems later, since the man employed as sales manager may not always be right for the job of marketing manager should further delegation from the top appear desirable. One tempting solution then is to leave the sales department undisturbed and to set up a planning section, reporting directly to the chief executive. This avoids some of the personnel problems inherent in change, but is usually ineffective because the planners tend to be left on a limb and denied the immediate feed-back that contributes so much

to realistic plans. At the same time divided responsibility for the profitability of the total marketing operation can lead to lack of motivation and
direction down the line.

The early appointment of a marketing manager to whom the entire
marketing function is delegated should imply recognition of the importance
of the planning role, and its close association with field activity. He will,
of course, be left with the problem of indicating clearly to his colleagues
in the accounts and production departments when he is speaking as an
objective planner and when as chief salesman. This is unlikely to be
achieved successfully on every occasion, and a role which places this twofold responsibility on one man is not an easy one to play. Good marketing
managers are therefore scarce and a great deal of care is needed to select
the right man.

This consideration serves to sharpen the argument at the next stage.
Granted that we have a manager in charge of the total marketing effort,
does he have under him planners and actioners[1] distinct from each
other or teams comprising both, divided by, say, product or geographical
area? The broad considerations that favoured integration at marketing
manager level could be considered equally valid at all stages, while from
the opposite point of view, the obstinate fact remains that two different
types of activity are involved and not everyone is equally good at either.

It is, therefore, valuable to look closer at the respective merits of separation and integration of 'planners' and 'actioners'. These can be summarised as follows:

|  Integration | Separation |
| --- | --- |
| *Advantages* | *Advantages* |
| Ensures that plans made will be fully understood and exe-cuted with enthusiasm. | Enables selection of right man for each job to be made more easily. |
| Improves communications from planner to sales force and feed-back from the field. | Planners can operate without undue pressure from individ-ual sales situations. |
|  | Actioners can spend more time in the field directing operations. |
| *Disadvantages* | *Disadvantages* |
| Personnel suitable for plan-ning function may not have line management qualities and vice versa. | Planners and actioners may not see eye-to-eye and communication blocks may be set up. |

[1]The word 'actioners' has been coined to describe those personnel with the marketing
junctions aimed directly at the customer.

| | |
|---|---|
| Short-term line management problems tend to take precedence over time-consuming planning activity. | Split responsibility may result in lack of involvement by either side in the success of the operation as a whole. |
| Immediate field reactions and customer difficulties may distort long-term product planning. | Customers may get insufficient attention if they do not fit planned parameters (i.e. there is a danger of the bureaucratic approach). |

These pros and cons might seem fairly well balanced, and organisations exist where each method has proved successful. In terms of Figure 10.1. it has been possible in some cases to thicken the line separating planning and action, and in others to remove it altogether. It is, in consequence, feasible to indicate the circumstances that might lead to a decision in one direction or the other.

If we start from the approach that has to be made to the customer, this may be organised by:

● Area – with sales teams covering a fixed geographical territory.
● Product – with separate sales teams for each major product line.
● Market – with sales teams for each category of customer.

There may also be a combination of these. Every marketing manager has to decide which method will be adopted, and this applies to small companies just as much as to large, although we may then have to read 'salesmen' for 'sales teams'. The optimum approach will be dictated by customer considerations, e.g. how many there are, how they are spread, how homogeneous is the market; and by product considerations, e.g. how similar are the products in application? what specialised knowledge is involved in selling them? are they sold to the same man in an organisation or to different men?

When a decision has been reached on the method of representation, the question of support services and the planning function tends to fall into line, although there are no rigid rules that can be propounded. If the sales force is to be organised on a regional basis, selling 'across the board', the establishment of a head office marketing planning department would seem a natural step to take. Organising on a market basis, again provided that a complete range of products is to be offered in each market sector, also favours a separate planning function. In the case of product divisions, there is much more room for argument and the issue may turn on size. Large units may be considered almost as companies in their own right, big enough to provide their own planning, forecasting and research within the division itself. This type of organisation is, however, outside the scope of a chapter where we are more concerned with companies with limited resources, which may nevertheless decide to organise their selling by product division. Here there may be a conflict between the benefits of employing a professional marketing planner to serve the needs of all divisions and the concept of the division as a dedicated task group in charge of its own destiny. Most divisions start small and the participants in the pioneering stage tend to be involved in all aspects of the business. They are unlikely to see fine distinctions between planning and action or to respond favourably to planning decisions taken outside the division.

This highlights three problems. The first is whether at any stage the concept of product divisions is easily compatible with a separate planning function. The second is how to ensure that planning takes place within the division if it is decided to include it. Lastly, there is the peculiar problem of new ventures which have no place in an entirely divisional organisation.

It might in general be said that as a form of marketing organisation, the product division has many deficiencies. It is for the most part company, not customer, orientated. It can lead to a duplication of selling effort and a dispersal of the overall marketing image. Nevertheless, it is adopted by perhaps the majority of companies with a wide range of products, and it has many advantages when it comes to training and motivation of sales personnel, and to communication within its own structure. It prevents the growth of what might be called the 'wigwam effect', where every product is sold mainly to support the others, and above all it stimulates profit-consciousness. If it is considered that the division is a new company in embryo, eventually to stand on its own feet, then there is much to be said for adopting this form of organisation. These arguments almost automatically rule out the possibility of a fruitful relationship between the division and a separate planning department. The whole divisional rationale is undermined if marketing decisions cannot be made from within.

Planning within a product division then becomes the responsibility of the divisional manager, possibly with the assistance of a junior to handle the statistical work involved, and to conduct internal research. If the divisional manager is a professional marketing man there may be no problems, but it will be a constant task of general management within the company to see that the divisions are looking beyond the here and now, and sorting out their marketing objectives for the long term as much as the immediate future. There are, of course, some marketing functions that can be centralised even with a divisional structure if they are regarded as services to the divisions, and these might include advertising, market research and public relations.

If there is no central planning beyond these services, launching new ventures which do not fall within the scope of any existing division may pose some problems. The company marketing manager has himself to act as planner in these instances. This will be simple in the early stages since he will himself probably have fathered the project and will be willing to give it a disproportionately high degree of his attention until it is seen to be firmly established, but there is, of course, a limit to the number of new ventures that can be undertaken at one time. This leads in some of the larger organisations to the reintroduction of central planning in the form of a 'new products' team.

## Marketing Personnel

### Product Manager

We have discussed the separation of function between actioners and planners, without so far defining in detail the responsibilities of each. There will of course be no need to discuss the more traditional functions such as, for example, sales management. The comparatively recent emphasis on planning has produced some new positions which do merit attention if the organisation is to be effective as well as fashionable. The most important of these is the product manager. He can appear in any of the types of organisation so far discussed, but is perhaps most common in the regional or market-based structure. To him, the marketing manager delegates the functions of product planning, forecasting, market research and the assessment of new products within a carefully defined area of responsibility. In the consumer field, the job can appear as brand manager with a strong slant towards sales promotion and advertising. An example of a product manager's terms of reference in an industrial company is shown in Figure 10.2. Such a position can be enormously valuable in co-ordinating the company's efforts product by product. The chief problem lies in measuring results. Clearly the product manager cannot himself achieve sales and cannot command the instant obedience of production, service and accounts departments. He is essentially a co-ordinator and planner and his achievement must lie in the attainment by others of the goals he has himself set. Generally, motivation is no problem with such a man, although frustration may be.

### Publicity Manager

When we come to consider more specialised functions, it is easier to assess whether or not appointments should be made. Advertising turns on the volume of work involved. If this is not great an outside agent can be appointed with the marketing manager as his main liaison point and with access to the product manager and the sales manager for details of products or campaigns to be promoted. If there are a number of promotional activities, exhibitions, direct mail, press advertising and above all a range of brochures to be produced then, the co-ordinating role can soon become too much for the marketing manager. A publicity manager could then earn his keep by ensuring that all promotional efforts are properly programmed, that the company as a whole is given a coherent image and that economies are made in buying advertising services. Such a man can easily save his salary by shopping around for print, direct mail and exhibition services.

## Market Research

Market research, even when outside agencies are employed, seldom appears as a major item of expense. Certainly it cannot be compared with advertising in this respect and the opportunities for savings are in consequence fewer. The problem of tackling market research in an organisation with limited resources is one of time.[1] There is no short cut possible here and the marketing manager has to immerse himself in research problems if he is to benefit from any survey made on his behalf.

### FIGURE 10.2.

### Terms of Reference – Product Manager

Reporting to: marketing manager

1. Staff

   To be responsible for staff functions delegated by the marketing manager.

2. Operational

   (a) To establish and maintain routines to keep under review the market standing and profitability of all products covered by the product line.

   (b) To recommend additions to, or deletions from, the product line, and modifications to existing products.

   (c) To review all new products or facilities offered as additions to the product line and all proposed modifications to existing products, to assess their market acceptability and profitability and to recommend acceptance or rejection accordingly.

   (d) After consultation with engineering department to classify all products within the lines as 'standard', 'non-standard' or 'special' and to keep the sales force informed of changes in product classification and of additions to or deletions from the range.

   (e) To keep the sales force informed of delivery periods for all 'standard' and 'non-standard' items.

   (f) To receive from regional managers all requests for 'specials' as defined. In conjunction with engineering department, to consider each request in the light of profitability, future sales potential and available resources and to accept or reject requests accordingly.

[1] See chapter 5 ('Marketing Research on a Small Budget').

(g) To render assistance as necessary to the regions on the product line.

(h) To keep the marketing manager continuously informed on competitors' prices, deliveries and product features and to recommend changes in policy.

(i) To produce a yearly sales plan for products within the line and to report progress quarterly or whenever required by the marketing manager.

(j) With the supplies manager to establish and maintain routines for forecasting and procuring stock items to provide optimum service with minimum stocks.

(k) To co-ordinate logistic support for all sales campaigns for products within the line and to ensure that all departments concerned are aware of the objectives and necessary action.

(l) In conjunction with the field sales manager to establish and publish to the sales force the features and benefits that should form the basis of our sales approach and to keep the sales force armed with full information on the relative merits of our own and competitors' equipment and service.

(m) To assist the field sales manager in the planning and execution of formal training courses, and to undertake regional training where necessary.

(n) In conjunction with the publicity manager to be responsible for all point-of-sale support for products within the line.

(o) To assist the marketing manager in the preparation of briefs for market surveys, and in the interpretation of market research data.

3. Advisory and Liaison

(a) To liaise with the publicity manager in the preparation of all publicity material related to the product line.

(b) To assist regional managers in formulating their forecasts by product line.

Recognition of the importance of research to any company working on a tight budget and contemplating fresh risks should serve to focus all the attention needed. If new ventures are few and far between there is no reason why the marketing manager or the product manager concerned should not do the desk work and proceed if necessary to the briefing of outside agencies. As the company grows, however, it might be worthwhile considering employing a market research officer specifically to undertake desk research and simple postal or telephone surveys with fieldwork where only a small sample is involved. The man or woman employed can then act as a liaison point with agencies when required.

*The Sales Force*

When the organisation for marketing planning has been created, it is necessary to monitor its relationship with the action function, in this case the field sales force. One of the potential disadvantages previously noted was the failure of communication between planners and actioners. Where the field sales force is concerned, the consequences of such a failure can be transmitted directly to the customer. It is possible to prevent, or at least limit, communication gaps by:

- Seeing that all marketing personnel work to clearly stated objectives which are common knowledge.

- Ensuring that planners explain the decisions they have made which affect field policy.

- Selecting people with the right degree of empathy to fulfil a planning and co-ordinating role.

- Ensuring that field reports are read by planners.

- Creating the physical conditions for communication, i.e. seeing that head office marketing personnel of all kinds are in the same location and that head office and field sales personnel meet each other frequently (and not only at head office).

Committees can be valuable as a means of getting planners and actioners together, but there are problems in obtaining 'grass roots' representation from the sales force. Unless the committee is to be unwieldy one or two people only have to be chosen to represent the field. Some principle of rotation will probably be preferred, but this leads to problems through lack of continuity. There is really no substitute for the rapport that the marketing manager needs to establish with all levels on both the planning and the action sides of his team. He can set overall policy and make it clearly understandable to all concerned, and if he is wise he will be approachable by anyone who has a positive point of view on where the marketing effort can best be placed.

To illustrate the way in which communication can be made to work successfully, one might look at advertising. This is an old bone of contention since few salesmen believe that they are getting enough advertising of the right sort. All too often advertising is prepared without reference either to the needs of the sales force or the plans of the product manager. The latter problem may be comparatively easy to remedy since although publicity has been classified as an action function, it can be located physically with the planners. To bring in the sales force at the design stage is more difficult, and it is not suggested that publicity material should be approved by a committee of salesmen. What is needed is that everyone who has a hand in producing an advertisement is acquainted with the realities of field selling, that any advertisement about which there is doubt is checked with field personnel, that every piece of publicity material finally approved is explained as well as issued to the salesmen in advance of publication and, above all, that the results are measured objectively through the appropriate field managers and relayed to the product planners concerned. If this seems to involve a great deal of effort, it should be said that communication does involve effort, and that what is true in this comparatively simple instance of advertising is even more true where controversial decisions involving product pricing, salesmen's incentives or territory changes are concerned. A great deal of the planner's work must remain unseen by the sales force, but that which is seen should be seen as clear, purposeful and relevant.

## Keeping Staff to a Minimum

It will be clear from what has so far been said that the introduction of marketing does not necessarily imply the establishment of a large staff of specialists. If the method advocated is followed, jobs are only created for clearly identified functions. There have been attempts to carry economies further than this and keep staff to a minimum by 'doubling-up' marketing roles, as when, for example, advertising is combined with market research. In general this type of economy is not advocated when the disciplines involved are so different from each other. It is hard enough to find a man competent at one job, let alone two or more, and where so few people are involved it is all the more important that each should be an expert in his trade. Until such time as a separate appointment can be made it is better for the marketing manager to control the function himself using outside help as necessary.

Real economies in marketing follow from an accurate identification of the jobs to be done, the selection of the right men or women to do them and a method of control which ensures the maximum effectiveness of each member of the team. These latter aspects will be discussed in the sections which follow.

## Selecting the Team

Once it has been decided to separate the planning function, suitable men have to be selected. This can prove troublesome since an error in the selection process can prejudice the whole concept. A company not previously organised for marketing may have few indications of the abilities of existing staff in the planning role, while the likely candidates may have insufficient knowledge of what is expected of them in their new capacity, and may show a tendency to retain previous job attitudes. There is, therefore, something to be said for looking outside the company, perhaps even for the marketing manager himself. There are, of course, pros and cons in any argument that may be made for recruiting from outside,[1] but at the very least an exercise of this sort should yield a standard of comparison against which existing personnel can be measured.

[1] See Peter J. Youdale, *Setting up an Effective Marketing Operation*, Business Books (London, 1972), chapter 2.

Unfortunately, there is still a problem when looking outside the company for ready-made planners in deciding what previous experience is relevant. The term 'marketing' has not always been used with discrimination, and in this field titles may be misleading. A man who has had the position of product manager may have been doing anything from field-sales management to advertising, with perhaps very limited experience of the type of planning that is in mind. So much will depend on the environment in which he has worked. A knowledge of the marketing structure and practices of as wide a range of companies as possible may help to get a fix on this rather elusive factor, but in many instances, the companies which have provided the experience will not have been particularly sophisticated either in their marketing organisation or their methods of selection. This is especially true of industrial marketing where engineering expertise may still tend to dominate at the expense of marketing skills. There is, therefore, no reason to assume that a man selected from outside will not require just as much training as the inside man with no previous planning experience, who at least knows the company's products.

In practice it is usual to be seeking qualities as yet unexercised, and the main benefit in spreading the net wider is simply to obtain a greater choice of candidates. There is no short cut to selection itself and the fact that we may be looking for only one or two men makes a thorough and painstaking approach all the more important.

*Profile of the Marketing Planner*

The method suggested here is considered to be the minimum that should be done to ensure a sensible choice for a key position. If the conventional terms of reference already illustrated in Figure 10.2. are examined, they may be elaborated to form a job description which lays stress on the key result areas, the degree of responsibility exercised, the resources employed, and the internal and external relationships involved. An example is given in Figure 10.3. It should be possible to determine the personal qualifications necessary to fulfil the role, and to list these in a 'man specification'. One way of doing this is shown in Figure 10.4. The important factor, however, is to have something in writing, rather than to interview candidates in the hope that what is being sought will somehow emerge more clearly in the course of discussion. It seldom does. The advantage of the particular method illustrated is that it is flexible and provides a guide rather than a rigid yardstick against which all candidates are likely to fall short. It is essential to ensure that only those qualifications that are really necessary are entered in the first column, since if any necessary qualification is not fulfilled, the candidate is automatically rejected. If he satisfies every point in the necessary column, all that remains is to balance those desirable qualifications he possesses against any contra-indications shown.

*Aptitude Tests*

An examination of Figure 10.4. will indicate that among the necessary qualifications for a product manager we have listed analytical ability. This, together with the temperament that allows objective thinking to take place, is a key factor in any marketing planning job. It is not, however, a quality that is easily measurable in the interview situation. If we are looking within the company, we may already have some evidence that would indicate the presence or absence of the ability to think clearly, but if we have to cast our net wider, we may be at a loss for clues that could enable us to compare one man's ability with that of another. For many of the other qualities, we can look at a man's past record, but here we need a finer tool to supplement our own judgement based on an essentially short meeting. One such tool is an aptitude test, and fortunately tests exist which can be related directly to the type of thinking needed in marketing planning. One of these is the Watson-Glaser Critical Thinking Appraisal.[1] This has been used in the selection of product managers and market researchers, although it is useful in the case of any job that requires clear thinking, and in addition, correlates well with the Otis Gamma IQ test. Its only disadvantage is that a qualified administrator is required. Its value is that it can detect the type of ability we are seeking, regardless of the academic history of the candidate. This widens our field of search considerably, which is just as well since there are still too few ready-made marketing planners available to go round.

FIGURE 10.3.

*Job Description – Product Manager*

1. Detailed terms of reference shown in Figure 10.2.

2. Key result areas
   (a) Orders received and profitability for all products under his control.
   (b) State of product training of sales force.
   (c) Accuracy of product forecasts.
   (d) Production of long-term marketing plans for existing and potential products within his line.
   (e) Success of sales campaigns directed towards products in his line.

3. Organisational relationships
   Reporting to: marketing manager
   No staff report directly to him.
   Liaison with:
   Chief engineer         — to advise on marketing, especially on new products.

[1]Available through the NFER Publishing Company of 2, Jennings Buildings, Thames Avenue, Windsor, Berkshire, which also provides a list of courses in test administration. Another organisation which provides assistance in aptitude testing is the Independent Assessment and Research Centre in 57, Marylebone High Street, London W.1.

Development manager— on new products.
Field sales manager    — on sales approach and product training.
Publicity manager      — on campaigns for products in his line.
Regional managers      — on marketing problems, specials and product
                         forecasts.
Area sales managers    — training in products in his line, assistance
                         with difficult jobs.
Salesmen               — training.
Systems engineers      — planning of jobs.
Supplies manager       — ordering and stocking.

4. Supervision of others
   No direct responsibility.

5. Span of decision
   (a) Major policy recommendations subject to review by marketing manager.
       Decisions on individual products or jobs are taken on own initiative.
   (b) Mistakes on major policy matters could take up to three years to
       discover and might take a further three years to correct.

6. Foreseeable errors
   As examples: Direction of development effort towards unprofitable ventures.
               Direction of selling effort to unduly difficult or unprofitable
               markets.
               Waste of operational resources in maintaining poorly con-
               ceived product offerings.
               Overstocking or understocking as a consequence of poor
               forecasting.

7. Personal contacts
   (a) Internal
       See 3 which lists the main liaison points. There are many more.
   (b) External
       Major customers and suppliers, market research agencies, publicity
       agents, competitors and trade associations.
   (c) Judgement needed
       Considerable judgement in evaluating likely suppliers and in dealing
       with customers and official bodies.
       Very high tact in co-ordinating interdepartmental effort on his products.

8. Control of plant and equipment
       Very little. Mainly confined to demonstration sets, etc. But his decisions
       have a bearing on investment in test equipment, tooling, racking, use of
       warehouse space, finished goods inventory, etc.

9. Commercial decisions
       Decisions affecting relationships with suppliers are strongly influenced
       by the product manager. Individual jobs are often negotiated on his
       advice. He usually takes the commercial decisions on disposal of
       obsolete equipment.

10. Authority over expenditure
       No formal authority, but see above for his influence on purchasing and
       stocking.

FIGURE 10.4.

*Man Specification – Product Manager*

| | Necessary | Desirable | Contra-Indications |
|---|---|---|---|
| Physical | Normal good health. Ability to carry weights up to 30 lbs. | Age 28–40 | Over 45 |
| Intelligence | 90th percentile with good numerical and verbal ability. | 95th percentile | |
| Aptitudes | Analytical ability. Capacity for technical appreciation. Good verbal facility and clarity of expression. Capacity for creative thinking. | | Mental block on technical subjects. |
| Attainments | Successful experience of direct selling. Administrative experience. | GCE 'A' level or above. | |
| Temperament | Objective thinking. Empathetic. Patient. Capable of conveying enthusiasm. | | Over impulsive |
| Domestic | Willing to reside near Head Office and travel throughout UK. | | Any domestic problems. |

If it is felt that when approaching the task of setting up marketing with limited resources the use of aptitude tests is inappropriate and the province of the big company only, it may be worth reminding ourselves that with a very small team we can afford less mistakes than the large organisation. A method that can provide virtual certainty on at least one important point at issue is therefore worth investigating further.

Of course, neither this nor any other similar test can predict whether a man will work. For that, a close examination of his record is indicated. Other factors, such as the verbal facility needed to communicate his ideas, are more easily checked. But by now, it will be clear that selection is a laborious process that cannot safely be curtailed. If, however, the effort required is forthcoming, the reward can be very great, since this is one way in which companies compete, and selecting a better team means that the game is already half won. It also enables a small company to score over larger rivals by spotting the good men that others miss.

## The Sales Force as a Catchment Area

There is an obvious advantage in selecting our team from inside the company whenever possible and for marketing positions, the sales force might be considered a natural catchment area. A salesman should have the ability to communicate and a feel for the realities of the market situation. Nevertheless, even assuming he measures up to all the necessary qualifications, there is still a need for caution in selecting a salesman for a functional role. If he is a good salesman, a great deal of job satisfaction may stem from a quick return on personal effort. The functional situation can prove frustrating to such a man since his results have to be obtained through others and may take a long time to materialise. He could, therefore, be looking for opportunities to turn his staff role into line control. A willingness to accept the functional position is essential, although this does not preclude further appointments into line management.

In industrial companies the choice may be between engineers with commercial leanings and salesmen with some technical understanding – or at least no mental blocks on engineering matters. If an engineer is selected, he would benefit from exposure to some selling before appointment in a marketing planning role.

## Career Structure

One of the problems of marketing organisation is the provision of a career structure. It might be argued that in a dynamic marketing situation expansion is bound to produce opportunities. Indeed, experience indicates that whatever skills we may possess in forecasting, few of us could predict the exact form our marketing department will take in two or three years' time. This uncertainty is, however, likely to have little appeal to a man deciding whether or not to move to a functional job, perhaps for the first time in his life. The possible opportunities he might consider attractive include promotion to marketing manager, or promotion to general manager of a division if a diversification becomes big enough to stand alone.

Naturally, the other personal qualities required for promotion have to be present, and some men will have reached their ceiling as product managers. There is, at least, the consolation that planning jobs retain their interest and it is fascinating and often very satisfying to watch the way in which decisions taken today will work out in practice over the years.

## Control

Having built his team, the marketing manager has to consider methods of control. It is here that he is likely to find himself at variance with his colleagues in other departments. Everyone accepts that sales management is an extrovert activity and however intellectual and cool-headed a sales manager may be, he has to some extent to accept the role others foist upon him. At least that gives considerable scope in management style, which can therefore be as free and easy as is required and is certainly likely to be persuasive rather than dictatorial in its general character. Marketing on the other hand looks to other departments more like an office function which should therefore be expected to follow firm administrative routines. These normally imply an emphasis on detail and encourage a tendency to frown upon 'mistakes' which can cost the company money.

The first thing that the marketing manager has to do is to disabuse his colleagues on this point. Marketing routines do indeed exist, but they are highly flexible, and marketing men who do not make mistakes will probably prove quite ineffective. In fact, a field sales manager has to adopt far stricter control of his men than would be appropriate in marketing planning if it is desired that the planners should think for themselves and think creatively. This means that the marketing manager has normally to run his team on a loose rein, acting more as an adviser, ready to give a second opinion when asked, than as a supervisor. How then can he exercise control and ensure that the team as a whole moves in the right direction at the right pace?

The problem is all the more difficult since functional managers cannot be measured directly by sales results. But it is still possible to set objectives and to work to a timetable. Some of these objectives will be non-financial (e.g. 'to produce a business plan for the next ten years by the end of April'), but others may have figures attached (e.g. 'to increase gross profit on products $x$ and $y$ to 45 per cent by the end of April'). In all such cases, it is essential that the planner has accepted that he can influence events to attain the agreed goal.

### Securing Acceptance of the Marketing Function

The establishment of a marketing department will obviously provoke reactions elsewhere in the organisation, and these have to be considered when it is decided to take this fundamental step. The sales force itself may react unfavourably when it is found that plans are being made which are at variance with its established view of the market situation. Close liaison work will help to prevent this getting out of hand. Nevertheless, to progress from merely correcting an anticipated bias to producing positive benefits from the relationship between planners and actioners requires more than this. Best of all is an early and demonstrable success. It is sometimes worth a minor shift in the order of priorities to arrange this.

As far as other departments are concerned, marketing has a co-ordinating role to play that requires the greatest tact if it is not to be taken as an invasion of their various spheres of influence. The marketing man is advised, therefore, to study the interests of engineers, accountants and production managers, to see what they want in business and to present his plans in the light of this.

As an example of what may happen, let us consider the introduction of a new industrial product. Engineering may have produced what they firmly believe to be the right product at a price that cannot be lowered. Production might want to get started as soon as possible to absorb surplus shop-floor capacity. Field sales will be happy to have an extra line to sell and may have customers ready and waiting. But the essence of the marketing concept is that the product should be right, not just for a few customers, but for sale in quantity over a period at a satisfactory profit. It should therefore have been made to a marketing specification and in spite of any 'engineering attrition' that may have taken place, marketing has to insist on its measuring up to the specification and passing any customer acceptance tests and field trials prescribed for it. Marketing therefore even at this stage has a right of veto which must be exercised whenever appropriate. Exactly how this may be done without too much heart-ache is discussed more fully elsewhere.[1]

It is an example of one of the points at which the marketing concept makes itself felt. There are of course many others (preparation of the annual budget, for instance) where marketing has a dimension to add to the activities of other departments. A good deal of effort will need to be extended to secure acceptance of the marketing role in all these areas.

### The Rewards of Marketing

In most companies which have genuinely organised themselves around the marketing concept, it would be hard to imagine how business could be conducted otherwise. The benefits for the smaller organisation are, if anything, greater than for the larger company, although it is unlikely to stay small for long. What has happened is that objective planning has replaced the hunch, and if this has been done well, creativity has not been stifled but directed more profitably. It is doubtful if any method can beat the inspired hunch in the early days of a business, but consider what happens if it proves successful. With success comes the need for administration, and much management effort is absorbed in handling the problems of growth. It then becomes necessary to defend the gains made and to allocate resources accordingly. So there is a danger that the next hunch may not come at all, or may fail through lack of management time, or that a second success may come only at the expense of weakening the position of the primary product. A marketing organisation enables product diversification to proceed without slackening of effort elsewhere.

Communication all the way from the design team to the customer and back is improved with the result that the sales force has greater

[1]For further reference see R. N. Skinner, *Launching New Products in Competitive Markets*, Associated Business Programmes (London, 1972), chapters 7 and 9.

confidence in the product, which is in fact more likely to be right. Morale is in consequence raised and is likely to be sustained for longer at a higher level. If a separate product planning section is created, then field management is freer to get on with the job of recruiting and motivating salesmen, and the company in formulating its corporate plans has the benefit of better market knowledge and more accurate forecasts.

## CHECKLIST

- Has a decision been made by senior management to adopt the marketing approach?
- Has a marketing manager been appointed to control both planning and action functions?
- Has a decision been made on whether or not to appoint separate marketing planners (e.g. product manager)?
- Have arrangements been made to purchase outside services for advertising, public relations or market research as appropriate? Have specialists been appointed for these functions where the work justifies?
- Have measures been taken to secure integration of effort between planners and actioners?
- Do the staff selected have qualifications related specifically to the new jobs created?
- Have management objectives been set for functional personnel?
- Has the position of marketing been established in all areas of activity related to product development and selling?

APPENDIX

# Polyart: A Case Study in Small Budget Marketing

By David Jones

Bakelite Xylonite Ltd (BXL) is a wholly owned subsidiary of the United States Union Carbide group. It has a turnover of over £50 million in the chemicals and plastics business. BXL can hardly be described as a small company – nor are its marketing budgets usually particularly limited.

However, like many sophisticated, multi-product companies, BXL spends substantial amounts on research and development; and BXL's board is asked from time to time by its R & D teams to give initial support to new products and processes which could take the company into new markets. The conception, birth and launch of Polyart, BXL's plastic paper, is a microcosm of the translation of R & D expertise into the market place. This has been achieved on a remarkably modest budget: for Polyart has been run as a pilot business within a modern chemical group. The initial success of Polyart has been due to the same small team which developed the process and the product.

## The Beginnings

The Polyart story, although essentially one of teamwork, also reflects the particular efforts of Dr Tom Watson, a scientist formerly in the R & D department of BXL's Industrial Products Division at Manningtree, Essex. BXL had decided in the mid-1960s to look at future markets where there was then little plastic in use, but where there might be volume potential. One such market was high-quality printing materials and the aim from the beginning was to develop a new business with a worthwhile profit potential. 'At the right time and at the right price we might even compete with paper,' was the objective. Watson was asked to develop a plastic paper – or in other words, to create a brand new business for BXL, based on the company's existing expertise in plastic film. 'By the first half of 1968, we convinced ourselves that we had a technically sound product', Watson recalls, 'after having completed extensive field printing trials with the new material.' The only way to evaluate the product fully was to put it on the market.

To get funds to set up a small production line, a convincing proposal had to be put up to the BXL board. 'I had market research findings which said that I couldn't sell for more than a certain figure – which was already two and a half times that of paper. I couldn't ask for more: and I couldn't sell for less.' Sanction for investment in a small-scale production unit (to the tune of £200,000 or so) was given. Watson could now test out this high quality premium product – which had to sell at more than twice the price of its only comparable rival, high quality printing paper.

Market research (mainly work carried out by trade associations and distributed to members) had quantified the existing volume and destination of high quality paper. Equally important, it had shown that the new product had to enter the market on the basis of value for money. One of the key properties of plastic paper, for instance, is that it is waterproof. Yet Watson was fairly sure that no one would pay a premium price for Polyart just because it was waterproof. 'Our knowledge of the plastics business convinced us that gimmicks were not sufficient.' Polyart had demonstrably to provide a range of properties which in total added up to a product for which people would pay extra.

He was now faced with two major problems. He had to break into an established market – high quality printing papers – with a brand new product, and he had to compete at a major price disadvantage.

On price, however, he was – and is – very sanguine. For some time Watson has believed that he has time and technology on his side. 'There are processing advantages,' he says, 'that we have in the extrusion of plastic film, which enable me to see how we could ultimately compete with paper. After all, paper's major breakthrough came with improved engineering techniques, that enabled manufacturers to build wider and faster mills. Just at this moment we are in the same area as paper was back in the nineteenth century. Our major breakthroughs have yet to come.'

But in 1968, Watson had to get Polyart off the ground. To appreciate his immediate problems, it is important to look at the market he was trying to enter.

### The High Quality Printing Materials Market

The printing and writing paper market in the UK at the beginning of the 1970s amounted to something like 1 million tons, and was expected to grow at about 4 per cent per annum over the next 5–10 years. Prices for wood-pulp based papers ranged from £130 per ton for the lowest grades to £450 per ton for the highest qualities. Prices were not expected to increase at more than 2 per cent per annum. The reason for this relatively low rate of price rise was that the efficiency of pulp manufacturers was expected to increase, while the cost of bringing timber to the mill would only increase by something like 2 per cent per annum.

This then was the size and price structure of the market that BXL was hoping to enter with plastic paper. The potential was some ten times that of other 'individual' plastic films, such as PVC sheet. What sort of product was he marketing, and what were its chances?

Polyart is a modified form of high density polyethylene (HDPE). It is a material which attempts to combine the properties of plastic film with the 'printability' of paper. It has some notable characteristics. It is extremely difficult to tear. It can be flexed repeatedly without cracking. It is waterproof. Finger marks, greasy spots, oil and so on do not affect its surface and can be easily wiped off. It has a smooth white finish, which permits brilliant colour reproduction. It can be printed and processed on standard machines including sheet-fed litho and letterpress (the basic processes of the traditional printer, large or small). In itself, to develop a product to be printed by sheet-fed litho was a major technical advance in both the plastics and paper worlds.

The applications for Polyart were clearly going to be as a printing medium where durability under arduous conditions was of prime importance. This meant maps, charts, brochures, leaflets, labels, trade catalogues, book covers, workshop manuals, point-of-sale material and posters. Since paper had a substantial price advantage, Watson had to educate and persuade customers that it really was worth paying a substantial premium for the durability of Polyart at the high quality end of the market. Laminated products and certain coated papers were vulnerable, perhaps amounting to 5,000 tons out of the 1 million tons which made up the printing and writing paper market – just 0·5 per cent.

As we have seen, BXL believed that long-term process improvements could ultimately bring down the price of plastic papers. But in the short run, too, there were some grounds for confidence that the price differential vis-à-vis conventional wood-pulp based papers could at least be maintained.

Among the polymers in current commerical use, HDPE has more potential than most for price improvements. There are generally admitted to be advantages still to be gained from economies of scale and improvements in processing.

In the long term, polymer prices would not merely maintain the differential but, it was felt, would actually fall relative to pulp prices. This would provide a sound base for plastic papers and could lead Polyart into new areas to compete with conventional papers. These would include such applications as children's picture books, art printing, inserts in popular magazines, timetables and mail order catalogues. This could add up to a potential market (including the earlier range of high quality paper uses first attacked) amounting to a maximum 100,000 tons – or as much as 10 per cent of the total market for printing and writing paper. To make a significant inroad into this 10 per cent was a worthwhile medium-term objective.

## Marketing Polyart

The basic strategy for Polyart was to educate and persuade customers that it was worth paying a premium for durability in the high quality market. For effectiveness and for economy Watson adopted a two-pronged attack. One was the use of backselling techniques, which would have the effect of inviting customers to approach Polyart for information and place orders with distributors. The other was the use of an existing sales network, in this case the conventional paper trade. BXL could provide the product and the expertise while an experienced merchant's sales force could do the legwork.

*Marketing Tactics*

Watson adopted the following mix of techniques:

*Backselling through advertising in the trade press, including the use of coupons.*

A typical exercise was an insert in *Advertisers Weekly*, *Design* and *British Printer*, which invited 40,000 readers to 'tear this and we give you a medal'. At a cost of £1,500 this brought in 600 enquiries.

*The creation of a very small, high level sales team.*

The three promotion executives in the Polyart team formed the spearhead of the BXL marketing operation. One concentrated on printers – which turned out to be very much a trouble-shooting role; one dealt with separate sectors of industry; while the senior executive dealt with advertising agencies and designers – who have the ultimate say on whether this comparatively exotic material shall be bought at all.

*The use of existing distributors' sales forces*

There was no sales force in BXL with the capacity or the expertise to sell Polyart to printers; and the potential UK market for plastic paper was not big enough to sustain an independent sales force. So from the very beginning it was evident that they would have to tackle the market through the conventional paper trade, through paper merchants.

But new products, however attractive, are costly to 'sell'. Could merchants, with a range of other products to sell, promote Polyart with as much 'muscle' as the rest of their lines? The previous two or three years had been difficult for the merchant trade and, as Watson says, 'in the early days no one is going to make a large profit out of Polyart'. Nevertheless in September 1972, Wiggins Teape paper merchants finally tied up a deal to sell Polyart. This meant that BXL's plastic paper was being sold by the subsidiary of one of Britain's biggest specialist paper manufacturers – an interesting combination of new technology with traditional marketing. In effect, this meant that promotion effort and expenditure within the trade was being stepped up.

As the operation grew, a business team (built round the section which had developed Polyart) was built up. This evolved into a production team of twenty-three hourly paid workers, a plant manager and his assistant, five research and development personnel, three promotion executives, a sales manager and a small office staff (including one with responsibility for European business) in addition to Watson, the business manager.

The team used the common services of BXL's Industrial Products Division: publicity, shipping and invoicing, computer, telex and maintenance engineering. Watson also had to bear a share of the Division's overheads. He was not convinced that a new business like Polyart should bear the share of overheads that such businesses carry; but he agreed that there is an immense area for debate over the allocation of overheads, whether on a full, greenfield or incremental basis.

**Overseas Marketing**

A major opportunity to expand volume outputs was in overseas markets.

*Europe*

From the moment of decision in 1968 to go into production on a commercial basis, it was realised that the European Economic Community constituted a major market. As in the United Kingdom, use was made of an existing sales network. Agreement was reached with the European Paper Group to sell Polyart in the Community. The Group is a consortium of merchants whose members buy in bulk but operate individually in their national markets – France, Germany, Holland and Belgium. The growth of sales has now allowed them to place regular contract orders.

The annual promotional effort behind Polyart began at a level of some £50,000. A proportion of this, of course, is spent by merchants; and half the total is spent in Europe.

*Japan*

Polyart's earnings come from further afield still. After two to three years, Watson felt he had established the name and product. BXL was a leader in plastic papers, and it is always difficult and expensive to break new ground. 'We went back to our sums,' he recalled. 'The background research and development had been continuing: we asked what were the deficiencies? What did we have to do?' Unlike the paper industry, the plastics film industry can make considerable increases in productive capacity for relatively modest injections of capital – say £100,000 or so. And an injection of this sort was made in 1970 to keep pace with sales growth.

It was now important to achieve further exploitation of the Polyart technology. Licensing offered an opportunity to achieve revenue, without the cost of direct selling, in remote markets. By this time, many requests to licence BXL's 'know-how' had been made, particularly from Japanese plastics and paper companies, who had a very large home market ready for development. Agreement was reached with Mitsubishi Rayon by which Mitsubishi was to build a large production plant of 2·5 metres width, with an overall capacity of approximately 3,000 tons per annum. Why Mitsubishi? 'We chose them from a long line of applicants,' says Watson.

As long ago as 1968 the Japanese Resources Commission had reported the need to develop an alternative to wood pulp as a raw material for the production of writing and printing papers. The main reason was the great increase in demand (allied to rising gross national product) which meant that the paper market in Japan was growing at something like 10 per cent a year. The Japanese were moving into a position where they would have to import 50 per cent of their wood pulp.

Simultaneously, the Japanese were trying to build up their petro-chemical industry. In 1968, the Resources Commission estimated that by 1978 they could be producing 3·5 million tons of plastic paper for writing, printing and packaging. The plastic paper industry in Japan accordingly shot ahead, backed in the usual Japanese fashion, by funds directed into this particular area of investment. Already two leading companies are marketing large tonnages of plastic paper not only in Japan, but throughout the world.

BXL's opportunity came with the decision by Mitsubishi to move into the market rather later than its competitors. Mitsubishi could buy time: and the Polyart process had reached just the right stage of development. Watson was able to exploit this commercially. The result has been not only that BXL has gained an important new source of revenue from Polyart, but that Mitsubishi in eighteen months moved into second place in the fast-growing Japanese plastic paper market.

### The Future

Watson has now moved Polyart successfully into the British, European and international markets (through Mitsubishi). He has done this by selected promotion (mainly backselling), by skilled technical support and by using conventional paper trade channels to sell a new product. BXL has not spent vast sums on promoting – or even manufacturing – Polyart. The business was still in embryo stage in 1973. It had to prove that it could pay for itself.

One day Watson might be earning 8 per cent return on capital – after tax – when Polyart has moved into production in the order of 10,000 tons a year. 'In that type of business,' he says, 'we would be shooting for big volume, low price, steady return on capital'. The skill and patience with which Polyart has been marketed so far should ensure its long-term success.

NB. Since this case study was written in mid-1973, BXL has moved further towards volume production. In July 1974 the group announced that a new plant at Clacton would replace existing facilities.

# Index